"It's all here—the hope, the enc want to hold when you're facir on. *Growing Forward When You Can't Go Back* women who feel lost and alone. Laurie's stories are heartwarming; her perspective of biblical women is fresh and unique; and her Blossom Tips are useful and creative. There's something for every woman in this book."

—Michelle Medlock Adams, award-winning author of more
than 80 books, including her latest, *Fabulous & Focused:
365 Daily Devotions for Women Who Work*

"Deftly weaving biblical truths with practical, accessible advice and compelling personal stories, Laurie Pawlik invites us into a life-changing journey forward from loss, disappointment, and brokenness toward healing, growth, and, ultimately, profound transformation. As you immerse yourself in Laurie's compassionate authenticity and allow yourself to soak up her grace-filled, real-life advice, you'll come away from *Growing Forward* with new hope—refreshed, renewed, and prepared to walk into the next season of your life."

—Michelle DeRusha, author of *True You: Letting Go
of Your False Self to Uncover the Person God Created*

"Laurie Pawlik has created a treasure of a book that will help women move out of the pain and despair they have experienced, into a season of wellness and growth. I love how she has blended her own losses with the studies of various biblical characters—you feel as though you have a friend with you as you all are journeying together. *Growing Forward When You Can't Go Back* is an excellent choice for individual reflection or small-group study."

—Janet Holm McHenry, bestselling author of 23 books,
including *The Complete Guide to the Prayers of Jesus*

"Laurie Pawlik is the master of writing with transparency and compassion, gently offering practical steps for healing our soul's soil from yesterday's pain. *Growing Forward When You Can't Go Back* is a must-read for those of us desiring to thrive and blossom in our next best season of life!"

—LaTan Murphy, author of *Courageous Women of the Bible*

"No matter what's happened in your past, it doesn't have to hold you back any longer. Laurie Pawlik offers practical tips for stepping forward into all that God has for you."

—Joanna Weaver, bestselling author of *Having a Mary Heart in a Martha World*

"Laurie is amazingly transparent as she shares from personal experience and Scripture, showing what it takes to grow forward when going back is not an option. If you are stuck, discouraged, or hopeless, applying the helpful tools shared in the Blossom Tips sections will enable you to bloom once more."

—Georgia Shaffer, professional certified coach, PA licensed psychologist, and author of *A Gift of Mourning Glories: Restoring Your Life after Loss*

"Laurie Pawlik has written a book for any woman who finds herself in a season of unexpected change or loss. She artfully weaves together the painful threads of her own life with biblical truth and the examples found in holy women from Eve to Mary. In the end, she not only shows us that growth is always possible, but gives excellent ways to enable and accelerate it in our lives. *Growing Forward* will inspire you to do just that."

—Bo Stern, author, teaching pastor, Westside Church, Bend, Oregon

GROWING FORWARD
when you can't go back

GROWING FORWARD
when you can't go back

Laurie Pawlik

BETHANYHOUSE

a division of Baker Publishing Group
Minneapolis, Minnesota

© 2019 by Laurie Kienlen

Published by Bethany House Publishers
11400 Hampshire Avenue South
Bloomington, Minnesota 55438
www.bethanyhouse.com

Bethany House Publishers is a division of
Baker Publishing Group, Grand Rapids, Michigan

Printed in the United States of America

Library of Congress Cataloging-in-Publication Data
Names: Pawlik, Laurie, author.
Title: Growing forward when you can't go back / Laurie Pawlik.
Description: Minneapolis : Bethany House Publishers, a division of Baker Publishing
    Group, 2019. | Includes bibliographical references.
Identifiers: LCCN 2018037399| ISBN 9780764232176 (trade paper : alk. paper) |
    ISBN 9781493417179 (e-book)
Subjects: LCSH: Christian women—Religious life. | Change (Psychology)—Religious
    aspects—Christianity. | Loss (Psychology)—Religious aspects—Christianity.
Classification: LCC BV4527 .P3869 2019 | DDC 248.8/6—dc23
LC record available at https://lccn.loc.gov/2018037399

Cover design by Greg Jackson, Thinkpen Design, Inc.

Author is represented by Books & Such Literary Agency

19 20 21 22 23 24 25   7 6 5 4 3 2 1

This book is dedicated
to you,
dear reader.

May you find peace and joy
in this season of your life.

May you grow forward
and Blossom
into who God created you to be.
With His Love,

Laurie
She Blossoms

CONTENTS

Contents

Contents

GROWING FORWARD

When a season of your life ends—whether by divorce, disease, or death—you know you'll never be the same. Everything is different! Your life has been uprooted, you've lost a huge piece of your heart, and you're left to pick up the pieces. You have to move forward but you just can't find the strength. You hope God has a plan for your life, and you're praying for a new beginning . . . but how do you actually start over?

In this book, you'll find encouraging and effective ways to walk through an unexpected season of life. Our stories of contemporary and biblical women healing and flourishing after setbacks and devastating losses will renew your hope and faith. The five practical Blossom Tips woven through each chapter will encourage, inspire, and strengthen you. The questions at the end of the chapters include an invitation to connect with me on my *She Blossoms* blog. You don't have to walk alone.

You'll slowly grow strong roots and see fresh blossoms in your life. Your heart will lift and fill with the peace of God, the love of Jesus, and the power of the Holy Spirit. You'll feel the life-giving warmth of the sun on your face. You will feel healthy, happy, and whole again.

"See, I am doing a new thing!" says the Lord. "Now it springs up; do you not perceive it? I am making a way in the wilderness and streams in the wasteland."[1]

A Peek into My Past

At last count, I've survived fifteen major losses in my life—starting from the day I was born. I grew up with a single Christian mom who struggled with nervous breakdowns and schizophrenia my whole life. My dad is Jewish, born and raised in Israel. When he landed in Canada in the late 1960s, he was planning to earn money, return to Jerusalem, and buy a business. Indeed, he moved back to Israel when I was nine months old.

My mother was hospitalized several times, unable to cope with episodes of severe paranoia and hallucinations. During her treatments, my younger half-sister and I lived in three different foster homes, plus a stint at a neighbor's house. Even when my mom was well, living with her wasn't easy; we often found ourselves wandering the streets in the middle of the night, and sleeping in cardboard boxes in alleys and on the front steps of churches.

You'll learn more about me as this book unfolds. I'll share glimpses of my journey through infertility and childlessness, a devastating family estrangement, a three-year stint of homesickness in Africa, and an attempted rape in my apartment in the middle of the night. You'll see how I grew through the setbacks, disappointments, and deaths. The best part? You'll discover how to weather the storms and droughts in your own life.

You will flourish and blossom in ways you never imagined.

Your Companions

In this book you'll meet a few of my *She Blossoms* blog readers. You'll see yourself in some of their thoughts and feelings. These women have survived many different types of losses; they are committed to healing, growing, and moving forward. Their honesty and companionship will fill you with comfort, encouragement, and hope.

You'll also meet ten women of the Bible as you've never met them before! Each chapter features a different woman and offers several lessons that apply to your life today. You'll witness their pain and grief, and learn how they flourished in a new season. You'll see how God changed—and still changes—situations that seem hopeless and endless, how He offers provisions and power when life feels overwhelming. Our biblical sisters loved deeply, lost tragically, grieved fully, and grew deeper in their lives and relationships. God was at work even when they couldn't see Him, and His plans turned out better than anything they could have imagined.

These ordinary women blossomed despite extraordinary heartache and loss . . . and so will you.

The Blossom Tips

Every chapter includes five Blossom Tips, to help you:

- Accept—and even embrace—a new season of life.
- Take small steps forward in practical, creative, delightful ways!
- Weave God's love and power into your heart, thoughts, and daily life.

Each Blossom Tip highlights a different part of who you are: spirit, heart, soul, body, and brain. This holistic approach will help you grow in specific areas of your self, life, and relationships. For example, if you want to increase your faith and deepen your walk with Jesus, you'll gravitate toward the Spirit Blossoms. If you need emotional healing, you'll be both challenged and comforted by the Heart Blossoms. If you want to explore the creative side of your personality, you'll love the Soul Blossoms; they're designed to help you express who God created you to be! You'll be physically strengthened by the Body Blossoms and intellectually challenged by the Brain Blossoms.

You'll find five Blossom Tips woven through each chapter, like roses climbing a trellis. At the end of the book, you'll have fifty practical ways to grow forward in your life. Every chapter begins with a peek into a difficult loss I or one of my readers have faced. Next, a biblical woman offers a unique, refreshing glimpse into her story, followed by a Blossom Tip for you to explore and weave into your own life.

This is the heartbeat of *Growing Forward When You Can't Go Back*. It may take you a chapter or two to adjust to this rhythm, just like it will take a beat or two to adapt to a new season in your life. Fear not! You are more nimble, resilient, and adaptable than you know—especially if you're following God's lead.

At the end of each chapter, you'll find five Blossom Questions for private journaling and group discussion. Take time to write through your thoughts and feelings; writing can be a powerful way to untangle painful emotions and experiences. Your "Blossom Journal" (a notebook of your choice) is the perfect place to explore your thoughts and talk to God.

Every chapter is accompanied by its own article on BlossomTips.com. I invite you to share your thoughts—big and little—with me in the "online garden" of my *She Blossoms* blog. You are welcome anytime.

Growing Forward in Your Life

Healing takes time, but time alone doesn't heal grief and loss. In fact, it's a myth that "time heals all wounds." Sure, injuries such as paper cuts and sprained ankles eventually heal, but time doesn't magically heal deep wounds. Appendicitis and cancer, for example, need therapeutic assistance and support. So do illnesses such as schizophrenia, depression, and anxiety. Those are physical, mental, and emotional wounds that require attention and care.

Grief is a similar type of wound. It's the emotional pain and suffering we experience after losing someone or something we love—including the loss of security, hopes, dreams, and expectations for the future. The feelings that accompany grief are often unexpected, confusing, and overwhelming. They can disrupt or even destroy our physical, emotional, and spiritual health.

As difficult as it is, loss must be grieved before we can move on and flourish. There are no right or wrong ways to grieve, but there are healthy ways to loosen unhealthy attachments to people or seasons of life. Accepting loss involves honoring the past and choosing to move into the future. This is growing forward when you can't go back, and it's what we'll do together as these pages unfold.

Where else to start but in the beginning? Let's dig up and air out a few family secrets, both in the Bible and in my life. . . .

1

Re-creating and Replanting with Eve

Families, created by God in the beginning, give us our first taste of love and joy. And, inevitably, grief! Sisters sail away, sons wander dark paths, parents wither and die. Husbands leave. Eve's response to her losses—and the Blossom Tips woven through this chapter—show us how to flourish even when we're no longer living in the Garden of Eden.

Sisters No More

"I haven't returned your phone calls because I don't want to talk to you," said my sister. "Not now, not ever. I don't want you in my life anymore." She hung up the phone.

That was the day—twelve years ago now—that I learned what "keening" means. I dropped to my knees and wailed like never before. Good thing I was home alone, in a little cottage on an island off the coast of British Columbia. If I'd been living in the city, someone would have called 9-1-1.

Now looking back on my sister's decision never to speak to me again, I see the signs I'd been ignoring for years. Our relationship was stormy from the beginning; we would often argue and not speak for months. We always seemed to be fighting about something, sometimes not even knowing what or why. She'd long ago stopped speaking to our mom. She refused to visit our dying aunt in hospice, and a few years earlier she had left her husband and two daughters. She was a leaver.

But I never dreamed she'd leave me. Not because of *me*, but because of our childhood. We grew up with a single schizophrenic mother, moved in and out of foster homes, didn't have a father. We had no other family; our grandmother and aunt both were gone. We were all we had, and I thought we'd be together forever.

But now it was just me.

The First Woman to Lose Everything

Eve is famous for being the first woman God created. She talked to the snake and chose to eat fruit of the tree that held secrets not hers to know. The Lord cast her and Adam out of the Garden of Eden, which shamed and devastated them. We may know this story well, but sometimes we overlook Eve's other experiences with death, grief, and letting go. Her experiences were heartbreaking. She was the first woman to lose her home, identity, and plans for the future. She suffered one son's death and another son's estrangement.

Eve was the first mother to:

- Grieve the death of a son.
- Agonize over her other son's crime of killing his brother.

- Feel the pain and shame of family estrangement.
- Rebuild a marriage wounded by grief.
- Heal and move forward without the support of a mom, sister, or aunt.

Eve's relationship with Adam—and with God—must have changed after her son Cain killed his younger brother, Abel. Her losses also changed *her*. Death and grief darken our perspective on the world, ourselves, our lives. Since Eve was the first woman God created, she didn't have female family members to lean on. She had Adam, but she didn't have the comfort and support of women who had experienced similar losses.

Worse, Eve didn't have the Holy Spirit's power, wisdom, and joy. She couldn't treasure God's words in Scripture because they weren't written yet. While Eve was on earth, she didn't know Jesus' grace, salvation, or love. And yet she found the strength she needed to keep moving forward. Perhaps her experience with God in the Garden of Eden sustained her through the pain. Maybe Eve recognized God's continuous, loving provision of food, clothing, and shelter even after she and Adam were cast out of the Garden. God did not abandon them. He promised that Someone would one day overcome the suffering and sin of this world.[1] Eve walked through the valley of grief, and I believe she emerged still believing in God's promises intact.

Our first Blossom Tip shows us how we can do the same.

SPIRIT BLOSSOM—
The Promise

Every general promise God made to believers in Scripture is for *you*—whether it was spoken to a king or prophet, queen or judge.[2]

A general promise is given by the Holy Spirit and applies to every believer in every age. You can trust God's promises for healing and hope, love and peace, joy and power. For example, Psalm 1:3 says we're like trees planted by rivers of water, yielding our fruit in season. When our roots are deep, we can draw on God's endless supply of strength, peace, and power.

A specific promise, in contrast, is given to a specific person in a particular situation. In Genesis 12:2 God promised to make Abraham and Sarah into a great nation. He doesn't promise that to everyone! But He does promise to bring forth good and wonderful things in our lives, even out of the hardest, driest seasons.

According to C. S. Spurgeon, "No promise is of private interpretation. Whatever God has said to any one saint, He has said to all. When He opens a well for one, it is that all may drink. . . . Whether He gave the word to Abraham or to Moses, matters not, O believer; He has given it to thee as one of the covenanted seed. There is not a high blessing too lofty for thee, nor a wide mercy too extensive for thee."[3] God's general promises of healing, peace, strength, and joy are freely available to us today.

What to Do

Find a Bible verse or passage that comforts, inspires, or strengthens you. Here's one of my favorites: "Come to me, all you who are weary and burdened, and I will give you rest," says Jesus in Matthew 11:28–29. "Take my yoke upon you and learn from me, for I am gentle and humble in heart, and you will find rest for your souls."

Copy the verse into your Blossom Journal (a notebook of your choice). Then rewrite the verse in your own words. Include your name. Here's my Matthew 11:28–29 rewrite: "Laurie, you no longer have to struggle with feelings of insecurity or worthlessness! Fix your eyes on Me and I will give you the love, identity, and freedom you need. Lean on me. We'll walk through this together. Fear not, for I am with you."

When you rewrite your verse in your own words, don't worry about how it sounds or looks. Just share your thoughts and feelings. Open your heart to God and imagine that He is speaking directly to *you* . . . because He is.

Not Best Friends Forever

My sister and I often joked about getting old together, sitting in our rocking chairs on the front porch reliving our childhood and remembering our favorite foster parents. Gary was the "Dairy King." When he made sundaes, we were allowed as much ice cream, chocolate syrup, whipped cream, and sprinkles as we wanted. Foster mom Beth had only one arm, yet she baked bread, planted a vegetable garden, and probably decorated a real tree at Christmas. I never found out. We didn't live with them that long.

When my sister unexpectedly cut me out of her life—without telling me why or what I had done wrong—I was blindsided. We'd been through so much together! Letting her go was horrible because I wasn't just losing a sister. I was losing part of myself, my identity, my past, and my future. I couldn't imagine a world without her. And what did it say about me, that my own sister didn't want me in her life anymore? I struggled with confusion, guilt, self-condemnation.

It took years to work through my insecurity and shame, to let go of who I thought I was and receive a new identity. It was an uphill battle because I fought alone. I refused to accept a new self-image from God because I didn't want to let go of my sister or the past. I thought letting go of her meant I would lose *me*.

And then, when I was finally ready to walk into a new season of life, I didn't know how.

How Eve Let Go

After the death of her son Abel, Eve had no choice but to let him go. Did she wail and keen? Did Adam comfort her? Perhaps he was the crier and she the comforter. Maybe they took turns, fumbling their way through their first experience with a death in the family.

Worse, Eve's eldest son, Cain, killed her younger son, thus committing the Bible's first recorded murder. She knew her boys were gifts from the Lord[4]—how could His blessings be the source of such grief? It was a devastating season for Eve as a mother.

Eve also had to accept the way God chose to punish her son. The Lord turned His back on Cain and cast him away from family and community. Cain was disgraced, destitute, estranged . . . and furious. "My punishment is too great to bear!" he said to God. "You have banished me from the land and from your presence; you have made me a homeless wanderer."[5]

Cain was Eve's firstborn child, still alive but just as lost to her as Abel. His relationship with God was destroyed, perhaps never to be healed. How did Eve cope with the pain? She didn't know about the stages of grief or psychological ways to recover from trauma. She couldn't read books about loss or bereavement. She had no counselors or doctors to call for help. And yet, she healed.

Before we discover how Eve recovered, let's do a little emotional healing of our own.

24

HEART BLOSSOM—
On the Mend

My first three months of counseling were delightful! My Christian psychologist, Nancy, was warm and kind. We spent hours happily chatting about me and my past. She was curious and encouraging; she hung on every word I said. But then she had this crazy idea: Let's do a little *work*. So we dug deeper and found the thick rock wall that protected my heart and prevented healthy relationships. Nancy helped me excavate the rocks and pull the thorns. I sweated, toiled, and bled my way through that wall. When I found my soft, scared little heart, it was still beating strong.

I had to trust that the seeds God buried during my season of counseling would eventually sprout and bear fruit. But first, there was work to do! I felt angry and sad about my childhood, ashamed of my flaws and failures. I wanted to quit counseling, but I knew I needed—and wanted—to recover from the past. So I kept digging up rocks, pulling weeds, planting seeds, and nurturing growth.

Behold! Glimpses of sunlight, fresh air, new sprouts. I started to heal and entered a new season of life. "See, I am doing a new thing!" God said. "Now it springs up; do you not perceive it? I am making a way in the wilderness and streams in the wasteland."[6]

What to Do

Recognize that no matter how smart and self-aware you are, you're also human. This means you can't see yourself objectively. You may be unaware of the obstacles holding you back, or unable to face the pain alone. A skilled counselor is a guide who can help you through difficult seasons by shining light on your path. You can learn how to grieve in healthy ways, perhaps by exploring your childhood losses or unresolved pain. Sometimes the past hinders the current healing process.

Schedule a three-, six-, or nine-month period of regular counseling sessions (a predetermined time frame will help you stay focused and committed). Expect counseling to be uncomfortable and even painful! If your counselor is truly helpful, sometimes you'll dislike your sessions. She'll hold up a mirror to your psyche, and you won't always like what you see. Trust the process. Remember that God is helping you heal and blossom into who He created you to be.

The Bittersweetness of Letting Go

When you lose someone you love, you need time to adjust to their physical absence. Life is emptier and quieter when that person is missing. Birthdays aren't as happy, Christmas isn't as merry, anniversaries aren't as special, and life just isn't as bright.

But it's the unexpected, often shocking, emotions that can knock you sideways. For instance, after my sister left I wondered if healing would have been easier if she had died instead of choosing to reject me. Her decision had sent me spiraling downward into confusion, guilt, and shame. I couldn't figure out what I had done wrong, and she never told me. I invented a million ways I was bad, selfish, unlovable, unworthy. My imagination cycled through endless loops of self-condemnation and self-loathing.

My sister is still alive—and I'm glad!—but we have almost no contact. I accept it. Maybe one day we'll be reunited. I hope so; I occasionally send her notes, saying I'm here if she wants to talk. Maybe she'll reach out . . . or maybe I'll never see my sister again. Either way, I have stopped torturing myself and I refuse to be buried in guilt and shame.

Counseling helped me start the healing process by digging through the rock wall around my heart. I learned about the aftereffects of a traumatic childhood and how to give myself comfort, compassion, and love. But counseling didn't heal my heart or become the bedrock of my self-identity. God took care of that.

God Let Adam and Eve Go

Imagine Eve's life after her son Abel was killed and God banished Cain! She and Adam were bewildered bystanders, witnesses to a violent eruption of pain and anger. After the dust settled, they must have felt helpless and shocked, unable to understand how their lives could have collapsed so suddenly and completely.

Their marriage would have permanently changed after they lost their children. Adam and Eve had to rebuild their relationship, perhaps fighting the temptation to blame each other for past parenting decisions. Letting go of their sons would have been heartbreaking; forgiving themselves for whatever part they played—real or imagined—must have felt impossible. Adam and Eve were stumbling forward into yet another new season of life.

God, too, felt the pain of this tragedy. "Listen!" He said to Cain. "Your brother's blood cries out to me from the ground!"[7] God *knows* and *feels* the anguish of death and separation. He grieved Abel's death and Cain's banishment just as deeply as Adam and Eve. Even before that, the Lord knew the pain of being left by a loved one. Adam and Eve rejected Him in the Garden of Eden. God's own Son, Jesus, also experienced the pain of rejection—as well as the physical agony of torture and death on a cross.

God understands the darkness and emptiness of loss more than we'll ever know. Jesus tasted death, but He didn't stay dead, cold, or buried. He always chooses life, in all its bittersweet depth.

As a Jewish man, Jesus celebrated many holy days and feasts. Some involved bittersweet symbols of new beginnings, as we see in the next Blossom Tip.

SOUL BLOSSOM—
Bittersweet

"Life is bittersweet," is what I learned in a Passover seder I shared with a Jewish family. We took turns reading the Torah aloud and eating foods that represented different aspects of the Exodus. This Jewish holiday—celebrated at home, around the table—is filled with foods that represent the Israelites' slavery and escape from Egypt.

We tasted bitter horseradish spiced with black pepper and vinegar, a symbol of the Jewish people's enslavement. A tiny sample with its sharp, stinging fumes brought tears to my eyes. Next was a thick, sweet honey-and-apricot jam that represented freedom from slavery. It was too sugary to eat alone.

So we combined them—the bitter horseradish and the sweet jam—on a dry matzo cracker. The flavors blended, textures meshed, aromas wove together as we tasted and saw that it was good. It was bittersweet . . . just like a deep, full, rich life.

What to Do

Find something tangible or physical that symbolizes the idea that your life is bittersweet. You might start with this poem:

The Weaver

My life is but a weaving
Between my Lord and me,
I cannot choose the colors
He worketh steadily.

Oftimes He weaveth sorrow,
And I in foolish pride
Forget He sees the upper
And I, the under side.

Not till the loom is silent
And the shuttles cease to fly
Will God unroll the canvas
And explain the reason why.

The dark threads are as needful
In the Weaver's skillful hand
As the threads of gold and silver
In the pattern He has planned.
— Author unknown[8]

Create or discover your own personal symbol of the bitter-sweetness of life. You might crochet an afghan, paint a sunset, or even cook a sweet-and-sour soup or sauce! Let it remind you that with great love can also come great pain. Dark nights are bitter, but the morning light is sweet. Both are in God's hands, and so are you.

Bringing the Past with Us

Recovering from my sister's rejection was like pushing a boulder uphill; every day it would roll down and I'd have to start over at the bottom. But the truth is I didn't really *want* to heal and move on. I just wanted my little sister back in my life. I

29

missed the good, fun, happy parts of our relationship. I often thought about our funny moments, secrets, and shared memories. Without her I felt alone and untethered. My sister took a huge piece of me when she left, and I wanted it back.

I resisted healing because it meant letting go of the past. Truly recovering meant moving forward into a new life without her; if I moved on, I'd lose my identity as the Laurie I once was. I'd lose the good parts of my childhood, the comforting feelings of family, love, and home. I gripped my pain because it was my only connection to my sister and my past.

But then I got tired of pushing that boulder uphill, day after day. It was emotionally and spiritually exhausting, and it left me without energy or motivation to start healthy new relationships. I began to realize I was basing my identity—and my future—on my sister's approval and love. If she accepted me, then I was acceptable. If she loved me, then I was lovable. Without her, I thought I was nothing.

I was basing my identity on the wrong relationship.

Growing Forward with Eve

Eve knew that God was in control of her and her family even when she couldn't see or hear Him. Further, her relationship with God changed as her life unfolded. Every birth and death she experienced must have affected how she saw, thought about, and talked to God. Eve's life changed in dramatic and shocking ways, but I believe she never doubted His absolute power and sovereignty over everything that happened in her life.

Consider, for instance, the different ways Eve referred to God. When her first son, Cain, was born she said, "With the help of the Lord I have brought forth a man."[9] In the Old Testament, "Lord" represented Yahweh or the Hebrew name of God

(YHWH). This is a sacred name, showing respect and reverence. However, when her third son, Seth, was born, Eve said, "God has granted me another child in place of Abel, since Cain killed him."[10] This use of the name "God" is more distant and general, perhaps indicating a shift in Eve's mindset.

The world and other people's choices—as well as her sons' unexpected death and banishment—changed how Eve related to God. She knew Him in the Garden of Eden, before sin pulled them apart. She knew Him in the dark, dry seasons of her life ... but she didn't let loss, pain, or grief stop her from trusting His goodness or accepting His gifts.

Why didn't Eve turn away from God, even when her life was as hard as pushing a boulder uphill? Perhaps she grew into a personal relationship with Him, and that changed everything. Maybe she made small but effective changes in her life that helped her heal and grow. A tiny tweak can make a huge difference in our lives, which our next Blossom Tip reveals.

BODY BLOSSOM—

Uphill Backward

If your faith—or your life—feels like a boulder you're pushing uphill, you'll love this tip! Drop the boulder; grab a pair of sneakers. My favorite way to exercise is by planting God's Word in my heart while enjoying a natural endorphin high. I listen to sermons on podcast while walking up hills. Backward.

Actually, I've progressed to *running* uphill backward (the trick is to lift your feet higher than usual and stay on the balls of your feet, not your heels). I started because of a hamstring injury, and discovering that walking uphill backward relieves pressure on my tendons, ligaments, and joints. It also strengthens thighs, calves, and bum muscles in ways previously unknown to womankind. Hello, calorie burn and weight loss!

What to Do

Schedule thirty minutes every day to walk, run, or bike with a God-centered podcast. Try to find an activity that surprises your body and metabolism, like walking uphill backward or pedaling backward on a stationary bicycle. Experiment with different routes and speeds. Add your arms! I incorporate overhead arm stretches and exercises while walking, to tone my triceps and biceps.

The more oxygen you have flowing through your muscles, heart, and brain, the happier you'll feel. Those natural endorphins are powerful, lasting long after you reach the top of the hill. While you're exercising, explore a variety of teachers, preachers, and worship music. I'm keen on Pastor Timothy Keller's sermons on podcast; his teaching is biblically sound and applicable to daily life.

Growing Forward

After ten years of pushing my boulder of guilt and shame uphill (backward), I finally dropped the burden and picked up the blossoms. As this book unfolds, you'll discover what helped me grow forward. You'll also learn how our biblical sisters and a few of my *She Blossoms* readers recovered from loss. Our experiences can help you work through your own difficulties, if you plant and nurture the seeds.

Remember that time does *not* heal all wounds! I didn't need a decade of boulder-pushing to recover from my sister's rejection.

It just took me that long to learn how to start and nurture the healing process.

How we choose to spend our time is the key to moving forward in a new season of life. I found counseling psychologically and emotionally helpful, but it didn't transform me spiritually. I needed to change how I saw myself and my past. I had to root my self-image and identity in God before I could truly flourish.

Your losses aren't exactly the same as mine. We aren't united by specific experiences of grief or pain. Rather, we're connected by something bigger and better: the hope, joy, and love only Jesus can bring! We're letting go of our expectations and plans for the future, trusting that we're in His good hands. We're allowing God to guide our lives. We're learning how to walk His way with yielded hearts.

It's time to move on and grow forward! Let's bid yesterday a warm farewell and tuck it away in our hearts. Our memories and loved ones will always be with us, but we won't let the past hold us back from becoming who God created us to be.

Eve Chooses Life in a New Season

"God has granted me another child in place of Abel," Eve said, "since Cain killed him."[11] Now, that is one healthy way to look at loss! Eve acknowledged God's power and providence. She accepted His gift of another child. At the same time, in the same breath, Eve was honest and authentic about her loss. She didn't try to hide the fact that one son murdered the other. She spoke the truth.

Eve wasn't in denial, she didn't hide from the past, and she didn't suppress or conceal her pain. She lifted her head, accepted God's blessing, and chose to move into a new season of life. Wow, Eve! No wonder her name also means "life-giving" or "mother of all who have life."[12] Eve experienced the full range of human emotion. She was blessed with the gift of life and she experienced tragic loss. Eve grieved and rose again.

Even though her relationship with God changed, Eve still saw Him as the Source of the blessings in her life. We don't know exactly how she worked through her grief and pain (did she roam the fields and gardens near her home? Weave tapestries with black and golden threads? Become the first grief counselor?), but we know she held on to God.

Eve chose to let go of the past, even if she didn't want to. She moved forward into a new season of life. In the last Blossom Tip of this chapter, Eve shows us how to honor yesterday and embrace today.

BRAIN BLOSSOM—
Fill-in-the-Blanks

Let's do a thought experiment with Eve's last words in the Bible. In Genesis 4:25 she said, "God has granted me another child in place of Abel, since Cain killed him." If we erase certain words, we can fill in the blanks with our own experience. Here's Eve's sentence when it's empty: "_____ has granted me _____ in place of _____, since _____."

Now let's fill in the blanks with our own thoughts. Here's mine: "God has granted me a new self-identity based on His love and grace in place of my old self-image of unworthiness and shame, since my sister chose to leave our relationship."

This helps me see what I learned and even gained from my loss. I'm honest about what happened, and grateful for my new identity. Here's another example from my life: "God has granted me time, energy, and finances in place of children, since my husband and I can't have kids because of infertility."

What to Do

In your Blossom Journal, write your version of this sentence: "_____ has granted me _____ in place of _____, since _____."

What has come out of your loss? You can fill in the blanks however you like; there are no right or wrong answers. This is your life, your losses and gains. Listen for God's still, small voice, and know He never subtracts without adding (though sometimes He requires you to wait on His timing). He delights in giving gifts; He *wants* to bless you with growth and fresh blossoms. See and accept His blessing even if it's not the person, possession, or future you expected. Don't overlook or underestimate even the smallest joys or faintest glimmers of hope. Those are the seeds and sprouts of new life.

Do this exercise five times, with different losses and blessings. Or you might choose to describe the same loss in various ways. Remember that death can bring unexpected life and fresh growth.

QUESTIONS *for* JOURNALING *and* DISCUSSION

1. **The Promise:** Which of God's promises resonate with you? How has He answered them . . . or are you still waiting?

2. **On the Mend:** How do you feel about talking to a counselor? If you sought counseling in the past, what were the benefits and drawbacks?

3. **Bittersweet:** Would you describe your life as a woven tapestry or a car wreck? What could you weave, knit, make, or bake to symbolize your life in the Weaver's hands?

4. **Uphill Backward:** How often do you surprise your body by exercising, moving, or stretching in different ways? What does your body need: rest or sweat, pampering or pushing?

5. **Fill-in-the-Blanks:** What benefits have emerged from your loss or pain? How do you feel about celebrating the blessings that arise after loss?

You don't have to walk through this season—or read this book—alone! Feel free to answer my questions and share your thoughts with me at BlossomTips.com/Eve.

Growing Forward

If your life isn't unfolding the way you planned or expected, you'll feel right at home in our next chapter! We're digging into Sarah's story. God didn't fulfill His promises the way she and Abraham expected, so she planted her own seeds. Her heart was in the right place, but her body and brain marched ahead of Him.

2

Sprouting with Sarah

Waiting isn't easy, especially when there's nothing else you can do. These Blossom Tips will help you wait with hope and peace; they're woven through my infertility story and Sarah's decision to fulfill God's promises in her own time, not His. Here, we discover how to avoid the temptations, trials, and troubles often found in the waiting place.

Bye, Bye, Baby

After seventeen years of friendship founded on camping adventures, road trips, hot debates, and cold spells, Bruce and I got married. We met when I was an eighteen-year-old waitress and he a twenty-one-year-old bartender at Chi-Chi's Mexican restaurant. Nope, it wasn't love at first sight over spicy chicken fajitas and frosty lime margaritas. In fact, Bruce and I lost touch for the three years I lived in Kenya.

But when we found our way back together, we knew it was time. Bruce was thirty-eight and I was thirty-five when we vowed to love each other for better or worse. Of course, we didn't have a clue what "worse" actually meant. We suspected kids would test our marriage, and they did . . . by stubbornly refusing to show up. Bruce was born ready to be a father; he's the youngest of six kids and wanted eight of his own. I, on the other hand, was a late bloomer. At thirty-seven, I finally felt ready to start our family.

We spent a year trying to get pregnant. Then a year of fertility tests. We assumed, and doctors confirmed, our age made it difficult to conceive—but we believed we'd have at least one child. God had brought us together after all these years, hadn't He? We're called to be fruitful and multiply, aren't we? *Of course* we'll get pregnant. We kept praying and consulting fertility experts, naturopathic doctors, and pregnancy books.

We also clung to the stories of infertile couples in Scripture who eventually celebrated baby miracles, like our biblical sister Sarah.

Sarah Marches Ahead

That she was barren is one of the first things the Bible says about Sarah (then Sarai). She conceived no children for Abraham (then Abram).[1] God promised them descendants as numerous as stars in the sky, yet she still wasn't pregnant after ten years of trying.[2] Sarah and Abraham were blessed financially, but piles of gold and miles of land can't fill a barren womb or an empty crib. Their hearts and hopes were crushed after ten years of not conceiving children.

In that time, family was the primary way Hebrew women gained their identity, self-worth, and purpose. Children were a sign of power, prestige, and position. Fertility was a blessing from God; barrenness was a sign of His disfavor and a source of deep grief.[3] And, as the wife of the tribal leader, it was critical that Sarah carry on their family name.

Sarah must have struggled with the feelings of failure, incompetence, and grief that often accompany infertility. Confusion and disheartenment are constant companions for many infertile couples, especially if they yearn for a family. Didn't God promise Sarah and Abraham numerous children? They were approaching their ninetieth birthdays; if too much time passed, they wouldn't be able to lift babies, much less chase toddlers or discipline teenagers.

Our biblical sister decided to make miracles happen instead of seeking God's will or patiently waiting (and waiting and waiting) for His plans to unfold. Sarah didn't appear to speak to God about having a family and fulfilling His promise to her and Abraham. Rather, she seemed to have shouldered a responsibility that wasn't hers—conception—by trying to fulfill God's promise through her own efforts.

Sarah is not alone. I, too, have forged ahead of God and made my own plans when waiting was hard. In fact, most of my biggest regrets are the impulsive decisions that I didn't take to God first! When I learned that Sarah is known by some as "The Woman Who Made a Great Mistake,"[4] I wondered if she ever had the opportunity to retreat and reflect. Were women's retreats a "thing" in Sarah's time? Today, retreats can give us a chance to reconnect with God, deepen our relationships with others, and even change the direction of our lives. This chapter's first Blossom Tip reveals the life-altering possibilities of retreating.

SPIRIT BLOSSOM—
The Retreat

How often do you refresh your relationship with God, yourself, and other believers? Women's retreats can nurture growth, replenish spirits, and strengthen communities. A retreat might revolve around a specific purpose, such as healing, studying a biblical book, or seeking God's will. Or it can highlight adventures that require faith and trust, such as zip-lining or rafting, songwriting, or preparing for a mission trip.

Retreats can change lives. For example, *She Blossoms* reader Carol (not her real name) experienced a life-changing weekend at a church retreat. She shared a cabin with a woman who was training a service dog, Barkley. He went everywhere with her, eventually becoming a canine companion to someone with special needs. Carol was enchanted with Barkley and the idea of being a volunteer puppy raiser for the first year or two of its life. Three months later, she took home her own puppy-in-training. That was six years ago, and Carol is still raising puppies for the program today. Her decision to attend the retreat gave her a new purpose in life.

What to Do

Look at the next two or three months of your calendar, and choose a block of time. Consult your church's website and see if a retreat or family camp is planned. If your church doesn't have an upcoming weekend away, search online for a Christian women's retreat center or conference.

Take a leap of faith and go alone! My favorite way to retreat is by attending women's weekends with church or spiritual communities I don't actually belong to. This way I can be alone (which I love, as an introverted writer) amidst a group of kind, faithful women. I read, write, and practice trusting God in unfamiliar places with different believers. Often I meet kindred spirits.

Another possibility is to create your own personal three-night retreat by visiting a destination you love or want to explore. Make time to look inward, upward, around, and ahead. Don't rush or fill your schedule. *Retreat.*

The "I" Word . . . Infertility

After years of disappointing pregnancy tests, Bruce and I added a new word to our vocabulary: *azoospermia.* His body didn't make sperm because of a genetic anomaly.

Hello, infertility.

We tried a variety of medical treatments. We welcomed prayers for healing and anointing. We were blessed under prayer shawls. One pray-er begged God to forgive us for the sins blocking His gift of children (though Bruce and I never believed sin was the problem). We discussed fostering and adopting children, but didn't feel drawn to either option.

We grieved the loss of our hopes and dreams of raising a family. However, while our hearts will always carry wisps and shadows of sorrow, we trust God's plan. In fact, I often wondered if God was *protecting* us from something. What if our baby was born with an infirmity I couldn't handle? What if my mom's schizophrenia was passed to our child? I believe God has good reasons for not favoring us with kids. And I savor the benefits of being childless! I have plenty of time and energy to write my *She Blossoms* books and blogs. I love my life in all its bittersweetness.

My willingness to move forward with peace and joy had a huge impact on Bruce. His heart was set on having a big family; the azoospermia diagnosis was shocking and almost unbelievable. Perhaps he would have wrestled longer with disappointment and grief if I hadn't embraced a change in direction. Bruce and I walked into a new season together, only later realizing how much of an impact we had on each other.

Another "I" Word . . . Impact

Infertility isn't just heartbreaking, it's confusing. God commands us to be fruitful and multiply,[5] and He specifically told Abraham and Sarah they would have more descendants than they could count. Of course Sarah grew impatient and tired of waiting! Infertility is emotionally, physically, and spiritually exhausting. Not to mention socially stressful—friends and family members are eager to hear pregnancy updates and share the latest fertility research, resources, and tips.

Maybe Sarah and Abraham told people close to them, or even the whole community, that God had promised them descendants as numerous as stars in the sky. Friends and family may have been watching and waiting for Sarah's belly to grow bigger, her appetite to increase, her servants to prepare the birthing tent. Maybe their homestead was already baby-friendly and toddler-proofed. After all, God's promise had come to them a decade earlier.

Instead, everyone just got older.

So Sarah made a strategic move to ensure that God's promise—and the desires of her heart—would be fulfilled. She thought she was being helpful. She acknowledged God in her decision but didn't appear to consult Him or pray for His will to be done. "The Lord has kept me from having children," she said to Abraham. "Go, sleep with my slave [Hagar]; perhaps I can build a family through her."[6]

Sarah's decision had a profound, permanent impact on the lives of everyone around her. She had no idea how monumental her choice was or how deeply it would affect her home, relationships, and future descendants. She had more influence than she realized! And so do we, as we see in our next Blossom Tip.

HEART BLOSSOM—

Your Impact

Your life has more impact than you may know! You have a direct effect on your family, friends, co-workers, and even people you haven't met face-to-face. Do you have a social media account, a blog, or an email address? Then you have power to influence others.

How you express your thoughts and feelings can affect someone's day—or even change a life. Your choices, actions, and words have an immediate impact on those around you. You can offer healing and encouragement in big and little ways. Or you can sow seeds of despair, discord, and disconnection.

Your emotions come and go, but your effect on the world will outlive you. Your actions may even echo in other people's lives and spirits forever.

What to Do

Pay attention to how your attitude, words, and actions affect others. This takes insight and a healthy awareness of boundaries. Your goal isn't to make everyone happy or solve their problems, it's simply to be aware of your influence. Watch how others respond to your choices, actions, and statements. Have the courage to admit that sometimes your impact is negative.

Don't rely solely on your own discernment. Ask a trustworthy friend or mentor for insight and guidance. Possible questions to ask include: "How do my words and behaviors affect you? Other people? How have I hurt you in the past? Encouraged you? What do you see in me that I'm unaware of?" Modify the questions as you wish. Give your friend time to think and pray before responding.

The Waiting Place

Carol, our volunteer puppy raiser in this chapter's first Blossom Tip, also struggled with infertility. She always wanted to be a mom but didn't marry until she was thirty. God promised her children, she believed, and she held on to that belief for fourteen long years. Finally, just after she turned forty-five, Carol and her husband celebrated the birth of their first and only son. He was conceived without fertility treatments, medications, or doctors. Just prayers and patience.

"Some seasons were harder than others," said Carol. "Christmas was painful because it's all about kids. Springtime was rough because pregnant women are everywhere. When I was trying to conceive, it seemed like everyone else got pregnant easily. My friends, family, and co-workers all seemed to have children . . . everyone except me."

Carol struggled through years of liminal space—that transitional time between two events. It's the time spent trying to get pregnant, waiting for medical test results, or even wondering if a lump or mole is cancer. It's waiting to see if you'll get the job, sell the house, or be accepted into the program. Liminal space is a period of uncertainty and yearning, wishing and hoping. It can be a time of sadness and healing, such as after a relationship ends. It might be a season of darkness, grief, loneliness.

Sometimes liminal space lasts a long time, as it did for Carol. Sometimes it whooshes by like a flower blooming while you weren't looking. Sometimes you can actually *see* growth! Little green sprouts poking through the soil, reaching for the sun. "See, I am doing a new thing! Now it springs up; do you not perceive it? I am making a way in the wilderness and streams in the wasteland."[7]

Sarah Waited . . . and Waited . . .

Like Carol, our biblical sister Sarah also experienced the liminal space of trying to get pregnant. Both women struggled with painful emotions, stress, and social stigma; both believed in God's promise that they would conceive. Both struggled with fear, doubt, impatience, and frustration. They had similar options but chose different ways to start a family.

Carol had two advantages that Sarah didn't. First, she learned valuable lessons about patience and perseverance from Sarah's decisions and experience with God. Carol found strength, hope, and wisdom by reflecting on Sarah's life. Second, Carol sought the power and presence of the Holy Spirit, available only through Jesus' life and death. This changed her heart, which changed how she moved through her season of waiting and hoping.

After ten years of trying to conceive, Sarah decided to pursue surrogate motherhood. It was a socially acceptable form of "fertility treatment" in Hebrew culture at the time. In fact, Sarah's family and friends may have wondered what took her so long! What on earth was she waiting for—a miracle? Giving her servant Hagar to Abraham seemed like a good idea at the time, and Abraham had no objection. Unfortunately, however, every record of discord and turmoil in Sarah's household was directly related to her choice to move forward without God's blessing.

Tempting, isn't it, to rush ahead of God? Especially in a liminal space that's painful, frustrating, or draining. Sometimes we need something to occupy ourselves with while we're waiting. Happily, our next Blossom Tip offers a delightful distraction.

SOUL BLOSSOM—

Jar of Blossoms

Maybe you're waiting for a season of trouble, trial, or testing to end. You believe God's promises but haven't received them yet. You know (and hope, and pray) change is coming, but when? How? With whom? Does God want you to keep waiting or act in faith? You're confused, frustrated. Tired.

You're standing at the threshold of what was and what will be. A new, fresh season is coming! This in-between time has the potential to transform you, if you trust and believe God is working all things together for your good. Liminal space can be rich with growth and rest, if you nurture it. Since you have no choice but to walk through this season, you may as well sprinkle it with joy, peace, and acceptance.

What to Do

Create a Jar of Blossoms. This is your container of big blessings and little joys, gifts, and giggles. When something good happens—whether it's a therapeutic massage or an Alaskan cruise—write it on a slip of paper. Plant it in your Jar of Blossoms. No need to get fancy (unless you're fanciful); your container can be a pickle jar, a wide-mouthed vase, or even a shoebox.

Every morning, pluck a Blossom from your jar. Every evening, plant a seed in it. Add happy memories, or even small objects that fill you with gratitude and joy. Include a symbol that represents a healed wound, forgiven hurt, or step forward. You can add pictures, cards, love notes, Scripture verses—whatever makes you feel blossomy! Make it a habit and it will lighten and brighten your liminal time.

Betrayed by Her Body

When Bruce and I were trying to conceive, we struggled with the emotional and psychological pain of infertility. But Bruce had an additional problem: He was disappointed and dismayed by his own body. Infertility affects men and women equally, but people often assume it's a female issue. So did we. His diagnosis was also shocking because azoospermia has no signs or symptoms. We were completely caught off guard.

Man or woman, it's heartbreaking to learn something so mind-boggling about yourself! Carol, who struggled with female fertility issues, felt betrayed by her own body. "I wanted to conceive so badly, but my body refused to get pregnant," she said. "All I wanted was to be a mom, ever since I was thirteen years old. I felt confident God would bless me with a child later in life . . . but the spring I turned forty-two was one of the worst seasons I experienced. My faith started to crumble. Other people knew how badly I wanted a baby, which made things worse."

Carol felt unworthy, insecure, and ashamed. She battled her body, struggling to take care of it so she could conceive while resenting it for not cooperating. She was constantly reminded that her body wasn't working the way it was supposed to, the way God created it to. She and her husband discussed fertility treatments but didn't feel compelled to proceed. Carol believed God would bless them with a baby, so they kept waiting, trying, and praying.

Sarah's Brain Raced Ahead

Sarah, too, was engaged in a battle with her body. She and Abraham assumed they were dealing with female infertility; they thought if he and young Hagar slept together, Hagar would conceive. The Bible says Sarah was past the age of childbearing,[8] so perhaps she wasn't ovulating or getting regular periods. She must have felt hopeless and discouraged at the thought of facing yet another menstrual cycle and preparing for yet another dalliance with Abraham.

Since Sarah's body was "the problem," she decided to find "the solution." So she proceeded without God, trying to create the life He intended by telling Abraham to sleep with her maidservant.

Indeed, Sarah's body appeared to be the reason God's promise of a fruitful family was unfulfilled. Abraham's sperm was healthy; Hagar conceived quickly. And Sarah was left out in the cold. Maybe her heart sank when she discovered Hagar was pregnant. Yes, Abraham's family would grow and God's blessings would flourish, but Sarah wouldn't be part of it. Yes, she could adopt and love Hagar's boy, but God's promise to *her*—Sarah—wouldn't be fulfilled.

Sarah lost faith in her body. She forgot God created her just the way she was *on purpose*. The body He gave her wasn't an accident, and it wasn't broken or defective. If she were here now, reading our next Blossom Tip, she'd be filled with fresh hope and faith. She'd see that her body was good, right, and perfect just the way it is.

BODY BLOSSOM—
Love Notes

I woke up last night at 3 a.m., fretting about my ailing dog (why did she throw up her dinner?) and my upcoming doctor appointment (what if I'm sicker than I think?). My thoughts could have erupted into a full-blown panic attack—but suddenly I realized that my brain is *astonishing*.

How clever, to imagine all the worst things that could happen! How diligent, to be working while the world slumbers! "Brain, how smart you are," I said. "You're alert and nimble when everybody else is snoring."

"Helloooo, what about me?" cried my heart. "I beat strong and true even while you sleep." And then my kidneys hollered, "Helloooo, remember us? We're brilliant at our job, too. And don't forget your lymph nodes, liver, and lungs!"

What to Do

Write your body a letter. Start with praise: Your eyes and brain are reading and comprehending these words, your heart is pumping, your lungs inhaling and exhaling, stomach digesting, hair growing. What about your nose that smells, tongue that tastes, ears that hear, eyes that see? Show your body some love and gratitude.

And face up to the downside. The sags, bags, and lags. Are you disappointed in your boobs or bottom, knees or nose? Write them a little note of love because they, too, deserve gratitude. Thank them for doing what they were created to do. It's not their fault they're getting old and worn out. Especially if you don't nurture them with healthy food, exercise, and rest. Isn't it amazing that you breathe without even noticing?

Leaving It with God

Carol struggled to leave her dream of getting pregnant in God's hands. She kept taking it back, fretting, obsessing, and lamenting. But despite occasionally straying off course and falling into a pit of despair, she faithfully held on to His promise.

"A lot of people asked me about adoption or fostering children, but I didn't want to take things into my own hands," she said. "I didn't want to step outside God's will because I really did feel like I had a promise from the Lord. I still dealt with longings and disappointment, but I decided to keep waiting and trusting. And God eventually honored my patience and faith with a baby."

Carol and her husband were blessed with a son. Bruce and I, however, experienced a different ending. Not happier or sadder, not better or worse . . . just different. We never felt that God had promised us children. We would have loved to have had a family together, but it just wasn't His will for us. My heart melts when I see a pregnant woman or hold a baby, but I'm sincerely happy for couples who are blessed with children. Their joy doesn't affect who I am.

God doesn't always answer our prayers the way we want. But if we knew what He knows—if we could see the big picture with all the pieces—perhaps we'd ask for exactly what we have.

Sarah Tried to Create a Miracle

After ten years of infertility, Sarah couldn't leave her dreams with God. She had to take control of the situation. In an Old Testament version of surrogate motherhood, Sarah gave her maidservant Hagar to Abraham. Hagar discovered she was pregnant, and her status was suddenly elevated to second wife. She was carrying the tribal leader's child! No longer just an Egyptian slave girl, she started treating Sarah with haughtiness and contempt.[9] This humiliated and enraged Sarah.

Sarah, perhaps regretting her decision to unite Hagar and Abraham, lashed out at Abraham. We don't know exactly why

Sarah blamed him; he did everything she told him to do. When Sarah complained about Hagar, Abraham said, "Do with her whatever you think best."[10] So Sarah treated Hagar cruelly, unleashing years of grief, resentment, bitterness, frustration, and regret. She let Hagar have it all . . . and it was so bad that Hagar ran away to the hot, dry Negev Desert. Alone. Pregnant. A penniless slave girl.

Sarah's choice to use Hagar and Abraham didn't just affect them; it had disastrous long-term consequences for their children, Ishmael and Isaac. Sarah's decision affected countless people in ways we'll never know. Of course, she didn't realize what would happen; we never know for sure how our choices will impact others.

All we can do is stay closely aligned with God, especially when we're starting a new season in life! Our next Blossom Tip—the last one in this chapter—will help us make decisions with wisdom, courage, and humility.

BRAIN BLOSSOM—
Smart Decisions

You are not alone if you've made an impulsive or emotional decision you later regretted. Maybe you even knew, deep down, that it wasn't the right choice. Maybe you were diverted by other people's expectations or opinions, or you thought it was your last chance at happiness. Perhaps you felt scared, lonely, or desperate. You saw your circumstances through the world's eyes instead of yielding and letting the Holy Spirit guide you.

Take heart! God redeems us, poor decisions and all. Don't allow past regrets to overwhelm your thoughts and emotions or weaken your future hopes and plans. Don't give Satan the satisfaction of tempting you into rumination and despair. Instead, seek wisdom and pursue His plans for your life.

What to Do

Learn how to make decisions that *aren't* based on your emotions, impulses, or yearnings. Instead, be thoughtful and faithful.

Here are a few tips:

- Reflect on your past decisions. How did you make good and bad choices?
- Talk through a current decision with someone trustworthy. Brainstorm your wildest ideas, hopes, and dreams! Discuss assets and liabilities.
- Explore the "why" behind an option you want.
- Examine how your decision may affect others—but don't let the unknown scare you.
- Consider waiting for a set time before proceeding.
- Decide "yes" and sit with it for a week. How does it feel? If it doesn't feel right, decide "no." Remember that "no" might also mean "not now."

Tell God what you *really* want, in your heart of hearts. Spend time in Scripture and prayer. Listen for His voice. Proceed slowly, one step at a time.

QUESTIONS *for* **JOURNALING** *and* **DISCUSSION**

1. **The Retreat:** When was the last time you went on a retreat—group or individual? Describe the benefits and drawbacks.

2. **Your Impact:** Who has had the biggest impact in your life? What did he or she do to be so influential?

3. **Jar of Blossoms:** Are you in a season of waiting, hoping, yearning? What are you dreaming of—realistic or not?

4. **Love Notes:** How has your body disappointed, frustrated, or even angered you? What are your least and most favorite body parts?

5. **Smart Decisions:** What was the smartest decision you ever made? What feelings, thoughts, people, or circumstances led you to that choice?

I'd love to hear your thoughts on Sarah's example of sprouting ahead of God, or anything that springs to your mind. Come, share at BlossomTips.com/Sarah.

Growing Forward

May you be filled with peace and faith as you walk forward boldly and humbly. Trust that if you knew what God knows, you wouldn't change *anything* about your life. May you always be prepared to meet Jesus in surprising places—like Hagar does in our next chapter.

3

Digging Deeper with Hagar

Unplanned and unpredictable storms blow through our lives, often dictated by other people's decisions, random circumstances, and tragic accidents. No warning or explanation! Sometimes they feel endless and destructive. The Blossom Tips woven through this chapter—and Hagar's life—show us how to flourish through it all.

Surprised by the Season

Growing up, I knew only a few things about my father: His name was John, he lived with his wife and children in Israel, and he was Jewish. And he loved to eat, especially fish! He introduced my mom to halvah, a rich Middle Eastern dessert. I didn't officially meet him until I went to Jerusalem when I was twenty-nine years old.

Born and raised near the Old City in Jerusalem, my father traveled to Vancouver when he was about twenty-five, in the late sixties. He had a purpose: to earn money, return to Israel, and buy a tire shop. He didn't plan on meeting my Christian mom or getting her pregnant. Nor did he plan on abandoning a baby girl in Canada or keeping us a secret from his family.

My mom didn't plan on the seasons she faced, either. She never thought she'd live in a home for unwed mothers, pregnant and alone. She didn't plan on meeting and marrying a different man, having another daughter (my half-sister), or getting divorced after three years. She didn't plan on raising two girls as a single mom—nor did she plan on living with nervous breakdowns and paranoid schizophrenia for the rest of her life.

And I never planned on spending my childhood moving in and out of foster homes, living on welfare, getting groceries from food banks, wandering from city to city and school to school. I couldn't wait to grow up so I could live on my own. When my stormy childhood season finally ended, I was happier than I dreamed possible.

That's the good news about bad seasons. They end.

Hagar's Seasons

Hagar was a female slave in a foreign land, facing circumstances beyond her control. Some were life-threatening! Jewish tradition says she was the daughter of the Egyptian pharaoh, given to Abraham and Sarah (then Abram and Sarai) to serve as a maidservant.[1] Abraham and Sarah were incredibly wealthy and had more livestock, silver, and gold than space to store it.[2] Hagar would have been one of many servants taking care of the chores, flocks, tents, and possessions.

When Abraham and Sarah moved back to Canaan, Hagar had to leave Egypt. Israel wasn't far away geographically, but it wasn't her home, family, or culture. Hagar's people bowed to the stone and wooden gods they made themselves, while the

Israelites worshiped the Lord God. Hagar wasn't raised believing in God, much less trusting Him to speak or guide her life.

When Sarah couldn't conceive the son God promised, she chose Hagar as the surrogate mother. This type of fertility treatment between servants and wealthy families was common back then, but it wasn't Hagar's decision. None of it was! She didn't choose to leave Egypt, work in Sarah's household, or serve in Abraham's bedroom. Hagar didn't choose to get pregnant with her master's child. Nor did she choose to have an untamable, uncontrollable, hostile son called Ishmael who fought with everyone.[3]

Hagar's life was controlled by people who didn't care how their decisions affected her. She was helpless and afraid, yet she kept moving forward through the storms and valleys. Her resilience reminds me of the different seasons described by the Teacher in Ecclesiastes, which is one of my favorite books in the Bible. Hagar's courage and determination inspired this chapter's first Blossom Tip.

SPIRIT BLOSSOM—
A Time for Everything

The book of Ecclesiastes contains one of my favorite passages:

> There is a time for everything,
> and a season for every activity under the heavens:
> a time to be born and a time to die,
> a time to plant and a time to uproot,
> a time to kill and a time to heal,
> a time to tear down and a time to build,
> a time to weep and a time to laugh,
> a time to mourn and a time to dance,

> a time to scatter stones and a time to gather them,
> a time to embrace and a time to refrain from embracing,
> a time to search and a time to give up,
> a time to keep and a time to throw away,
> a time to tear and a time to mend,
> a time to be silent and a time to speak,
> a time to love and a time to hate,
> a time for war and a time for peace.
>
> —Ecclesiastes 3:1–8

What to Do

Reflect on a few different seasons in your life. Start by writing the words "A time to be born" in your Blossom Journal. What have you birthed—babies, groups, community initiatives, creative or work projects? What has God birthed in your life that you didn't choose? An unexpected new season, perhaps, or a painful ending. Loss and death often contain the seeds of new beginnings.

Move on to the next phrase, "A time to die." What deaths have you experienced? Did you trust God through those seasons, or did you cling to the past? Explore different ways to walk through your loss and process the grief. Learn how to transition through the pain, and what it means to rest in Jesus.

Write your thoughts about each season in Ecclesiastes, or just select a few. End with "A time for peace." What does this mean to you, in your life today?

New Season, New Identity

Growing up without a dad had an appalling effect on my self-identity. Worse was living with a mentally ill mom who called me names, punished me physically, and yelled at me in public. Band-Aids everywhere, inside and out! I struggled to hide my shame and pain from friends, fellow students, and teachers. Believing they were perfect and happy, I envied their lives. I fluttered on the fringes of school activities and daily life, trying not to be seen.

Somewhere along the way I adopted a rather distasteful identity: worthless, unlovable, and bad. I based my self-image on my circumstances and family history, feeling inferior and alone. I kept people at a distance and hid behind walls of superiority and self-righteousness. I judged and condemned others to protect myself, often treating people like they were inferior or stupid. All to avoid feeling bad about myself.

Acting haughty and condescending was a coping strategy that helped me survive childhood. Unfortunately, it wasn't a smart approach to adulthood! I ruined several relationships before realizing that people don't like being treated like fools. So I learned how to be friendly and cooperative, but I still felt worthless and unlovable.

Slowly I realized my self-image was based on external factors: family background, body size and shape, income, education, job title, achievements. What I needed was a more meaningful source of identity. I needed a new perspective, a new heart.

Hagar's New Identity

Hagar's self-image and ego swelled with Abraham's child in her belly—and it changed how she treated others. Even her boss! "When Hagar knew she was pregnant, she began to treat her mistress, Sarai, with contempt."[4]

Hagar was no longer just an obedient Egyptian maidservant; she was the mother of Abraham's first son and heir. Her child would inherit the family's wealth, possessions, land, and servants.

This changed how Hagar saw herself, which affected her attitude and behavior. Perhaps she felt superior because she was treated with more respect. Maybe she was given lighter chores or extra time off. Perhaps she was moved to better living quarters. Maybe Abraham himself favored her because she was carrying his baby; perhaps he gave her the plumpest dates and sweetest raisin cakes. However it happened, Hagar's self-image puffed up and affected how she treated the people around her, including Sarah, who held the power.

Hagar's elevation of social status wasn't the problem. Women often receive work promotions, social resources, or other blessings without becoming proud. The problem was that Hagar's inflated self-image and ego was based on her new circumstances. Her status improved because of her body's ability to conceive, and she was filled with pride and contempt. Her ego turned her into a haughty and hurtful woman.

Our biblical sister Hagar fell into the trap of allowing her external circumstances and reputation to control her self-identity. Just like I did! And both Hagar and I had an encounter with God that changed everything. She met Him in the Negev; I met Him in our next Blossom Tip.

HEART BLOSSOM—
The Letter

A few years ago I participated in a Bible study that transformed my heart. One activity in particular had an immediate, powerful effect on both my self-identity and my relationship with God. It was a fifteen-minute writing exercise that invited us to picture ourselves the way God sees us, and write ourselves a letter from His perspective.

When I saw myself through God's eyes, my heart melted. I was filled with compassion, love, and kindness for the little Laurie who experienced terrible troubles. I saw myself as a little girl with ribbons and curls, bouncy and joyful! Precious, lovable, and worthy of God's attention. Naïve and vulnerable, whole and free, loved by Jesus. His heart and sacrifice healed that little girl's pain and shame.

My experience with God freed me from pride and haughtiness. I saw myself though His eyes; my heart and self-image was slowly renewed.

What to Do

Picture yourself through God's eyes. How old are you, and what do you look like? Where are you, and who are you with? How do you feel about yourself? What is your self-identity based on? What does Jesus want you to know? Take fifteen minutes to write yourself a letter from God's perspective.

You have a unique relationship with Jesus, so your experience will be different from mine. You may feel angry, sad, or lonely. Maybe you can't picture how God sees you. Perhaps you'll have more questions than answers, more confusion than clarity. It's okay. Don't judge or compare. Don't expect God to show up in a specific way. Take a deep breath and close your eyes. Let God reveal himself to you. Let Him reveal *you* to you.

Running Away from Home

I ran away from home when I was thirteen years old in a most unusual way: by calling Social Services and talking to a social worker. My previous foster care experiences hadn't just sheltered me, they taught me how to properly leave an unhealthy, abusive environment. I'd stayed in foster homes with compassionate parents, warm beds, well-stocked fridges, and school supplies. I'd already experienced—and wasn't eager to relive—the adventure of sleeping in hard cardboard boxes in cold back alleys of big cities.

At home, my mom was disintegrating physically, emotionally, and mentally. She kept going on and off her medications because she didn't like the uncomfortable and often harsh side effects of the powerful antipsychotic drugs. She was also trying to hold down a teaching job while raising two preteen girls as a single mom. Her struggle led to all sorts of unpleasant experiences at home, ranging from physical abuse with wooden sticks to culinary abuse with margarine sandwiches on stale white bread. I couldn't live with her anymore, especially since she was getting better at hiding her illness from the doctors.

So I called a social worker for help. I knew there was always the possibility of ending up in an unhelpful or even abusive foster home. I'd heard they existed, but I knew staying with my downward-spiraling mom was riskier than running away.

Risks All Round

Hagar, too, chose the risky option of running away. When she went from meek servant to expectant mother of Abraham's heir, her ego grew bigger than her brain. She became an outspoken thorn in Sarah's flesh by treating her with contempt. Sarah responded so harshly that Hagar fled to the Negev Desert.[5]

Perhaps Sarah was lashing out in grief and regret. After all, it hurts to be around pregnant women when you're struggling with infertility. Watching another woman grow round with your husband's baby would have been heartbreaking. Sarah was still barren even though God had promised them a family. Her body was a failure, her spirits low. She wrestled with her identity as a woman because she couldn't achieve what even a servant could: getting pregnant. Using Hagar as a surrogate mother had seemed like an effective way to build a family. Risky, perhaps, but since Abraham had no objection, why not? It was a culturally acceptable practice.

After Hagar conceived, Sarah faced unexpected consequences. First, her servant now had an intimate, beautiful, permanent bond with Abraham. Second, Hagar's growing bump was her husband's baby, heir to a great nation. Third was the straw that broke the camel's back: Hagar treated Sarah with haughtiness.

So Sarah handled Hagar roughly—badly enough to make Hagar run away. It was risky to be a female slave in a foreign land, and even riskier to be pregnant, single, penniless, and wandering the Negev Desert. Hagar was facing an almost guaranteed death for herself and her unborn baby. It would take a miracle to save them.

A foolish risk, or a faithful leap? Our next Blossom Tip explores both.

SOUL BLOSSOM—

Risk

Leaps of faith feel risky, *and* they help you get closer to God. Pursuing a unique possibility—especially in a new season—changes how you see yourself and God. Taking a risk is your chance to learn how He leads and where He might want you to go next. When you avoid new possibilities, your heart grows cold, your spirit dull, your life flat. You can't grow without taking risks, much less blossom into who God wants you to be.

Maybe you're stuck in a rut or struggling to let go of the past. Maybe you refuse to accept invitations or new ideas because you're uncomfortable or afraid. Or maybe you think taking a risk has to be big and scary, like quitting your job or moving to Africa. On the contrary! A step of faith can be as simple as inviting a co-worker to lunch or joining a new church group.

What to Do

Create a one-week plan of small daily risks. For example, on Monday wear more colorful clothes to work. This is risky because you might attract attention or feel judged. Tuesday, start a conversation with someone you see often but don't talk to. Risky, because you're reaching out to a stranger. Wednesday, take a fitness class you've never tried before. Risky, because you'll feel uncomfortable and won't know what to do. Thursday, apologize to someone for losing your temper or breaking a promise. Risky because you're admitting you were wrong. Friday, invite friends over for a meal you've never made before. Risky, because it may not be perfect and you might feel embarrassed.

Reflect after each risk. How did God show up? Consider taking bigger leaps of faith that require you to rely on and trust God more than before.

No Going Back

Calling Social Services when my mom was sick was risky; I didn't know if they'd grant my request and put me in foster care

64

or leave me with her. They wouldn't remove me if they thought I was exaggerating or lying about her illness. And if they left me at home, life would get worse! My mom was already furious that I called for help. There'd be consequences for calling a social worker, and I'd be the one to pay.

The social worker did a home assessment a couple of days after I called, and he removed me and my sister that evening. I wanted and needed to leave my mom, but it was hard. I felt guilty for calling Social Services and terrible that she'd be alone. I loved her. Living with her wasn't bad *all* the time, but she was too sick to take care of us.

But there was no going back. I had to keep moving forward and trusting that everything would be okay. At the time I didn't have a close, personal relationship with God—though I believed in Him—because I was caught up in day-to-day survival. I didn't understand the concept of walking with Jesus through scary valleys and dark nights. I loved going to church, but I thought God was neutral about me. I knew He wouldn't *object* to my presence, but I didn't think He desired or sought it. He could take me or leave me.

I never realized God actually saw and cared about me, just like He saw and cared about Hagar.

Turn Around, Hagar

Running away was risky because Hagar was legally required to stay with Abraham and Sarah. As a servant, she was considered a piece of property, without rights. Slaves couldn't just up and quit their jobs, especially when pregnant with the master's child! But Hagar's risk paid off in an unexpected way. She saw God and was seen by Him. She didn't happen to accidentally run into a disciple or apostle; God actually sought her out in the Negev Desert. The angel of the Lord called her by name.

Hagar wasn't looking for God, and she certainly didn't expect Him to initiate a conversation, but the angel of the Lord found her exactly where she was.[6] He knew her name, her position, her need for love and support. Hagar was at the lowest, loneliest point in her life, and nobody cared. God *saw* her, and this had such an impact that from then on she called Him "the God who sees me."[7] Hagar gave God a new name.

By calling her "Hagar, slave of Sarai,"[8] God reminded Hagar of her identity in that season: She was a servant with a job to do. It wasn't the best or most enviable job in the world, and she didn't love her work. But at that time in her life, Hagar had to turn around and go back. God told her to return to Abraham and Sarah[9] because, like it or not, that season of her life wasn't over.

Turning around doesn't seem like a tip for blossoming in life, does it? Unless, of course, you create a healthy "Turn-Around" that changes your perspective.

BODY BLOSSOM—
Turn-Around

Physically, the biggest "Turn-Around" I've experienced was in my relationship with food. My struggle with bulimia started after I left my mom when I was thirteen, and ended thirty years later. I couldn't fight the compulsion to binge and purge heaps of cookies, ice cream, and potato chips. My counselor taught me that overeating was a substitute for love, security, and comfort. It also distracted me from grief and pain. Purging was necessary to relieve the physical discomfort of all that food, and to get rid of the calories! Counseling didn't cure me, but it did help me understand eating disorders.

The Letter in the Blossom Tip listed earlier healed my heart and broke the emotional power of addictive eating. However, I still needed practical ways to change how and what I ate. My Turn-Around was discovering how immediately and directly certain foods affect my mood and energy levels. I started to notice how sluggish, tired, and heavy I felt after eating certain foods, and how horrible I felt after a binge-and-purge episode. Paying close attention to my body was a crucial step to healing.

What to Do

Evaluate your eating habits. What foods do you eat most often, and how do they make you feel? Do you feel energized and light after eating, or dull and lethargic? If you feel full and sluggish, then you're not eating nutritious food. Your first step is simply to notice how you feel after you eat. Pay attention to what you ate, how it was cooked, and what was on top or inside. Writing down the specific details is even more powerful.

Experiment with different Turn-Arounds in your kitchen. Start by observing how each food or eating habit (e.g., overeating while watching movies) affects your energy and self-image. Remember that God blessed us with food for nourishment, energy, and enjoyment! He gives us delicious food because He delights in mouthwatering flavors, tastes, and textures. Simply notice if and when you use food for escape, comfort, or entertainment. Don't pressure yourself to change. Simply bring what you learn to God.

Fainting Away

Calling Social Services when I was thirteen was a risk that paid off. It was hard to leave my mom, but I landed in a safe place. I didn't reach out for professional help again until I was thirty—and that experience was so scary I passed out cold.

When I was teaching in Kenya, my school offered free counseling services for staff. Since I'd never talked to a counselor before and figured I had a few issues to iron out, I figured it would be fun. Why not?

I fainted and fell to the floor the morning of my first appointment. I'd been standing at the back of the library during morning staff devotions. Dan, the math teacher, was closing our time in prayer. Suddenly the room shifted, and darkness started to fall. The floor rose and smacked me on the side of my face. Someone said, "Laurie fainted!" Dan didn't miss a beat; he smoothly transitioned into a prayer for me and my health. I opened my eyes to see a circle of faces staring down at me.

Thinking it was just a coincidence, I didn't mention it to my counselor, Nancy, right away. When I finally told her, she said the decision to work through painful past experiences has a powerful effect on our bodies and minds. Talking to a counselor awakens spiritual and emotional forces that can create massive shifts in our psyches and lives. Fainting was my body's way of coping with anxiety and fear of the unknown.

Yes, it's risky to grow forward! But it's riskier to stay stuck in the bud.

Hagar Saw the Light

The first time Hagar left Abraham and Sarah, God told her to return. She went back to them—not because her circumstances changed, but because her heart did. Hagar's encounter with God convinced her of His loving, trustworthy plans for her life.

Hagar and Ishmael lived with Abraham for about thirteen years, until after Sarah gave birth to Isaac. A miracle baby after all that time of waiting! Genesis 21 tells us that when Isaac was weaned, a skirmish broke out between half-brothers Isaac and Ishmael, and Sarah told Abraham to banish Hagar and Ishmael. Again, Hagar found herself wandering alone under the desert sun, defenseless, and responsible for her son.

Hagar and Ishmael finished the water Abraham provided, then collapsed in fear and despair. Not wanting to see Ishmael die, Hagar put him in the shade under a bush and went a little distance away, crying. God heard Ishmael's cries and opened Hagar's eyes. Behold, a water well, right in front of her! She quickly gave Ishmael a drink, and God walked with them through the wilderness.[10]

God didn't shield Hagar from hardship; He showed her a way through it. Hagar couldn't see water at her fingertips because she was blinded by tears, fear, and despair. Her body was exhausted, her spirit beaten, her heart broken. Hagar's sorrow suffocated her faith and she forgot God's promises. She and Ishmael would have died alone, but God again brought her through the darkest season of her life. "See, I am doing a new thing!" the Lord tells us. "Now it springs up; do you not perceive it? I am making a way in the wilderness and streams in the wasteland."[11]

This chapter's final Blossom Tip will help you see something Hagar couldn't: a map of resources that can carry you through even the most trying times.

BRAIN BLOSSOM—

Mind Map

Sometimes we can't see the help or support that is right in front of us. We're blinded by grief, fear, or pain. Sometimes Satan distracts us or convinces us we're helpless and hopeless. Sometimes we feel unworthy, unmotivated, or uncertain about the kind of support we need. Often we think we can push through a difficult season alone. Sometimes we're too proud or afraid to reach out and ask for help.

Seeking and accepting emotional, medical, or financial support is hard. It's risky because it involves being honest, vulnerable, and humble. It's painful because some thoughts and emotions are easier to avoid or suppress. Nevertheless, getting help is the healthiest way to navigate a difficult season of life. It also honors God because it involves seeing and accepting the resources He has already provided.

What to Do

Create a "mind map" of possible sources of support in your life. Take a big piece of unlined paper and draw a circle in the middle. In the circle write "Resources." Draw four lines extending from it, like sun rays. Draw four circles at the end of each ray. Write the following in each circle: *People*, *Places*, *Extras*, and *God*. Voilà! Already you have four helpful resources.

Draw four lines extending from each circle and list your possibilities. For example, in my "People" circles I'd write *Bruce*, *Ann*, *Ruth*, and *Rosie*. In "Places" I'd write *church*, *library*, *forest*, and *social services*. In "Extras" I'd write *journaling*, *jogging*, *drawing*, and *listening to podcasts*. In "God" I'd write *power*, *wisdom*, *inspiration*, and *joy*.

Add more ideas to your circles, such as *co-workers*, *online groups*, *books*, and *neighbors*. What type of support do you need now? Reach out with gratitude and humility. One day you'll be in a position to return the favor.

QUESTIONS *for* JOURNALING *and* DISCUSSION

1. **A Time for Everything:** What was your most treasured time of life? How do you balance letting go and moving forward in a new season?

2. **The Letter:** How, when, and where do you experience God most deeply? Does seeing yourself through His eyes affect your identity?

3. **Risk:** What's the biggest risk you've ever taken? Knowing what you know now, what would you do differently?

4. **Turn-Around:** How do your eating habits affect your day and mood? On a scale of one to ten—with one as "destructive" and ten as "healthy"—how would you rate your relationship with food?

5. **Mind Map:** What are some surprising sources of support and comfort in your life? How do you feel about asking for help?

Share your thoughts with me on BlossomTips.com/Hagar. How are you coping with this season in your life?

Growing Forward

Your future may contain unpredictable, even frightening, seasons of change and growth. Together we'll make our way through the falling leaves, broken branches, and crashing trees. In our next chapter we'll explore creative ways to build new nests in different forests with our biblical sister Naomi.

4

Uprooting with Naomi

Two journeys to Israel are interwoven through the Blossom Tips in this chapter: Naomi's return home and my pilgrimage to meet my father. Our adventure starts in a forest, with a parable about a brave Mama Bird and a wise lumberjack. Even birds find themselves unexpectedly rebuilding their nests....

Mama Bird and the Lumberjack

When they are thrown out of the nest, birds are forced to fly before they feel ready. This forest parable tells of a lumberjack who saw Mama Bird building her nest atop a tall tree. He knew the tree would be felled soon and she would lose her home and babies. So the lumberjack pounded the base of the tree with the back of his ax. Mama Bird was disrupted and had to find a new home for her nest. She chose another tree and started to rebuild.

But that tree, too, was slated for a fall. Again the lumberjack pounded the tree so hard that Mama Bird—getting annoyed— was forced to fly away. She landed on a third tree. The lumberjack returned and shook his head. This wouldn't do. Again, Mama Bird was forced to leave. Confused and cross, she built her nest atop a high rock, sheltered from the sun, rain, and wind. She was finally safe, never to be shaken.

The tallest, healthiest trees can look good on the outside: thick green leaves, sturdy branches, pretty apple blossoms. We nest there, not realizing they're diseased, unsuitable, or slated for a fall. We refuse to leave, unable or unwilling to see the spots of rot in the trunk, beneath the leaves, under the soil. We ignore the wilting branches, patchy fruit, bitter root.

Sometimes we're shocked and confused when we're pushed out of a tree. Sometimes we don't know what the lumberjack knows.

Naomi's Tree Came Crashing Down

Ever since we were cast out of the Garden of Eden, humans have been searching for home, security, and comfort. Jesus' own ancestors, Naomi and her husband, Elimelek, were looking for a better life when they left Israel and went to Moab. If ever there was an unhealthy tree, Moab was it! Moab and Israel were enemies. Moabites worshiped and sacrificed children to cruel gods such as Moloch and Baal. In fact, Moabites were seen as cursed and forbidden to settle in Israel.[1]

Naomi and Elimelek left Bethlehem in the dark days of the Judges,[2] attempting to build a better life for themselves and their sons, Mahlon and Kilion. They fled Israel's famine and struggle, choosing to go back toward the same wilderness God delivered their ancestors from years before.[3] Naomi and Elimelek planned to return to Israel. They sojourned, which means they traveled briefly, but they never went back. They didn't just leave their families, traditions, language, and land in Israel—they left the Lord. If they wanted to assimilate into Moabite culture, they couldn't openly worship God. Their sons' marriages to Moabite women further entrenched them in foreign customs and traditions.

Naomi and Elimelek's brief sojourn became a permanent way of life. If they felt God calling them back to Israel, they ignored Him. If they remembered the lively echoes of Shabbat, as described in this chapter's first Blossom Tip, they pretended not to hear.

SPIRIT BLOSSOM—

Nose-to-Nose

My imagination takes me to Galilee two thousand years ago. I'm a little girl playing with wood blocks on the floor of a warm, exuberant Jewish home. It's Friday after sunset; family and friends are gathered for Shabbat. A fire crackles in the fireplace, and every inch of the long, low table is crammed with dishes of fresh olives, fig cakes, lentil stew, fish, oils and vinegars, warm bread, and red wine. Often, someone—usually Peter—raises his goblet and shouts, *"L'Chaim!"* To life!

Tonight Jesus is reclining between John and Mary of Magdala, dipping a piece of bread in a bowl of stew. He takes a big bite as He laughs at Peter's fishy tale of the 140-pound tilapia that capsized the boat and escaped the net. Jesus' eyes linger over the people at the table . . . and He sees me. Maybe He remembers me from before, when He beckoned but I was too shy. This time, I promise myself, I'll go if He calls.

What to Do

Imagine yourself in this boisterous Jewish home. You smell smoked fish, feel the warm fire, hear laughter and songs of praise. Jesus is celebrating Shabbat, relaxed and happy. He's with people He loves—and you're one of them. He sees you and His face lights up! He waves you over. As you shyly draw near, He reaches out and pulls you toward Him. You climb onto His lap and find yourself nose-to-nose with Jesus.

Behold His dark brown eyes, curly black hair, and beard. Deep lines around His eyes and mouth, courtesy of the sun and sea. Put the palms of your hands on either side of His face and squeeze. Jesus with a fish mouth! He laughs, and your body relaxes against His. You put your small arms around His neck and hug Him. You feel the warmth of His neck and hear His breath. Your heart beats with His. Everything fades away as your eyes close and you rest. You're glad you came when Jesus called.

My Sojourn to Israel

The first time I went to Israel I was twenty-nine and on a mission to meet my dad for the first time. I'd sent him a letter six weeks earlier, not wanting to catch him off guard by showing up unannounced. I suspected his wife and kids didn't know about me, and I wasn't sure he'd want to meet. He didn't respond to my letter. Did he even get it? Did he read or speak English? What if he rejected me or denied being my father? I was a stranger, the illegitimate daughter from his past. I had no idea what to expect.

When I arrived in Israel, I found a thousand reasons not to call my dad. I was in the Holy Land, after all! I had to explore all the biblical places I'd read about: the Mount of Olives, Galilee, Bethlehem, Nazareth, En Gedi. I expected to see my dad everywhere I went. I didn't know what he actually *looked* like, of course. I could only imagine.

When I finally summoned the courage to pick up the phone, the first thing my father said was, "What took you so long to call?" We met in the lobby of the King David Hotel in Jerusalem. We immediately recognized each other because I look just like him. I look so Jewish, in fact, that both Jews and Palestinians think I speak Hebrew. I look more like my father than his other children, but I'm the outsider.

Naomi's Life as the Outsider

In Moab, nothing happened the way Naomi planned. Her husband, Elimelek, died, leaving her alone in a land of people who worshiped cruel gods. Her sons, Mahlon and Kilion, ignored God's command not to intermingle with pagan neighbors. They married Moabite women, Orpah and Ruth. Both couples were childless. Ten years later Mahlon and Kilion both died, and Naomi buried her husband and sons in a foreign land.[4]

Not only was she crushed in heart and spirit, Naomi was a vulnerable older widow. She had no family and didn't belong in Moab. She decided to return to Israel even though she was an outsider there too. But Naomi had no choice: Her tree had fallen; her nest was crushed, and her flock had flown away. She had to let go of the dreams that died with her husband and sons. She had to move forward.

Naomi heard that God was doing good things back home in Israel, and she had nothing left to lose. The seven- to ten-day journey to Bethlehem through the desert and across the Dead Sea would have been arduous for anyone, much less an older widow traveling with her two daughters-in-law. Orpah and Ruth may have become family to her, but they were still Moabite women. They'd be seen as pagans in Israel, outsiders cursed by God. Naomi was returning with foreigners who might be demeaned and rejected, perhaps even abused.

It was a risky move for a bereaved, bitter widow. Naomi was facing a major life change, and she didn't have our Blossom Tips to ease the transition.

HEART BLOSSOM—

Surprise!

Today during my writing break I turned on the radio. The first words I heard were, "How do you deal with a life transition that doesn't work out?" It was a talk show about people whose lives fell apart after a major decision. Tazmeen, for example, moved to Africa with her husband and children. She had dreamed of writing a novel set in Tanzania; her husband wanted to work as a pilot. Their children were young, so they would transition smoothly. Everything was set! Until they actually moved to Africa.

Tazmeen's daughter fell off a chair onto the concrete floor and suffered a serious head injury. Her husband couldn't find a job; they struggled financially. Then he got hit by a bus and was hospitalized for days. Nothing turned out the way Tazmeen and her husband planned.

What to Do

Take stock of what you've recently lost or experienced. Maybe your heart is shattered by an accident, death, or painful family decision. You're devastated because you have to rebuild your life or home. You feel lost and unsure, scared and alone. But instead of resisting, what if you choose to accept and even embrace your new life? What would it feel like to welcome, rather than resist, the season God is allowing you to experience?

"When things don't go as planned, you have to embrace it," said Tazmeen.[5] "Maybe it wasn't your plans that went wrong. Maybe your expectations were unrealistic, and the way things happened was right." Tazmeen's daughter survived the head injury, her husband healed, and her book was eventually published. Even though nothing went as planned, it was transformative. "Our life in Africa turned out beautifully," she said. "It wasn't what we expected, but it was amazing."

Meeting My Dad's Wife and Kids

After we met at the King David Hotel, my dad invited me to stay with him. He didn't approve of my hostel accommodations in the Christian Quarter of the Old City, so I found myself meeting his Canadian wife and three teenage children at their home. His wife is from Vancouver, where my dad met my mom thirty years earlier. In 1971 my stepmom did what my mom couldn't: moved to Israel and started a family with him. Talk about building a nest in a whole new forest!

Before meeting my dad, I struggled with anger and resentment. It wasn't fair that he abandoned me and didn't offer any support while I trudged from one foster home to another. It wasn't fair that I had no emotional, social, or financial resources to help me through university. It wasn't fair that I had to teach myself everything about growing up.

Meeting my dad was good, but it didn't heal the pain. In fact, meeting him had the potential to make me feel *worse*. He was an excellent husband, provider, and father to his other children, giving them everything they needed to succeed. Yay for them! Boo for me. Meeting my Jewish family didn't make me bitter about how unfair life can be. It didn't make me better, either.

Naomi's Root of Bitterness

Naomi knew she had to leave her old life in Moab. The past was over; it was time to trek back to Israel. Naomi was moving forward, but she didn't have hope or faith in God's plans for her future. On the contrary, she was eating bitter fruit. "Call me Mara, because the Almighty has made my life very bitter," she said. "I went away full, but the Lord has brought me back empty."[6]

Like Eve in the beginning, Naomi lost two sons. Unlike Eve, Naomi had female support and companionship. She had Orpah and Ruth, two daughters-in-law who loved her and were willing to give up their lives in Moab for her. They wanted to go to Israel with her, not because of her gifts and blessings, for she had nothing, but because they were loving and loyal daughters. But Naomi, blinded by grief and bitterness, couldn't see or receive their love.

She told them, "Go back, each of you, to your mother's home. May the Lord show you kindness, as you have shown kindness to your dead husbands and to me. May the Lord grant that each of you will find rest in the home of another husband."[7] Another heartbreaking loss; all three women wept openly. Naomi, Orpah, and Ruth were cutting the last remaining ties to their past life together.

Ruth, however, had a different idea! Not only did she know the true meaning of love and devotion, she actually embodied it. Ruth was a friend who would help Naomi blossom in unforeseen ways.

SOUL BLOSSOM—

Friends

Throughout Scripture, God encourages us to build and maintain connections with like-minded folk. We need fellow Christians for emotional health, because it's not good for us to be alone.[8] We need each other for protection; a cord of three strands is not easily broken.[9] We need each other for connection[10] and unity; we're adopted into God's family, and in Christ we form one body. Each member belongs to all the others.[11]

But remember: Your friends' habits and character traits rub off on you. Choose your friends with care. Do you often feel emotionally or spiritually exhausted after spending time together? Reevaluate your relationship. You needn't feel bad or guilty if you're unable or unwilling to nurture a friendship. You have a finite amount of time and energy; focus on building and nurturing healthy, life-giving relationships. Remember that even Jesus was closer to some people than to others.

What to Do

Do a "friend inventory." Are you regularly spending time with kindred spirits, people who share your beliefs and values? Can you share your true thoughts and feelings, and accept theirs? Do your friends challenge you to grow in healthy ways? How do they affect your relationship with God? Are your relationships sprinkled with laughter, connection, and deep conversations about difficult topics?

Schedule regular phone calls and in-person activities with your friends. Nurture your relationships by telling your friends what they mean to you. Take initiative in organizing visits. Note birthdays, anniversaries, important events in their lives. Cling to the companions who are important to you, like Ruth clung to Naomi.

Better, Not Bitter

I wasn't bitter about not having a dad growing up. Rather, I was consumed with self-pity and inferiority. I also thought people with two parents had everything: comfort, love, security, health, and success. It wasn't until I made a close friend at university that I realized bad things can happen behind beautiful doors.

To protect her privacy, we'll call her Bunny. She had the cutest rabbit tattoo on her neck! Her dad was a surgeon, her mom a school principal. Her brother and sister were finishing their university degrees. Bunny didn't have to worry about tuition, books, groceries, or rent. She spent holidays with her family, sometimes meeting them in Maui or Paris. I yearned to be part of her smart, respectable family. Oh, the security and comfort.

I was confused, though, because Bunny was miserable. She wore black clothes and dark makeup, pierced her nose and eyebrows, tattooed her body with cute animals and scary skulls. She was irritable and depressed, taking medications for various health issues. She struggled through university—not because she couldn't handle the coursework, but because she couldn't handle *life*.

Never did I learn why Bunny was so bitter, but it slowly dawned on me that having a two-parent home didn't guarantee happiness, success, or security. Nor did it ensure a healthy identity. I also learned that adapting to life's surprises and storms isn't about who our families are or how much money we have. It's about *who*—not what—we trust through the unpredictable seasons, when we're thrown out of the nest and forced to rebuild.

Naomi Chews the Bitter Root

After traveling on the road to Bethlehem for some time, Naomi told Orpah and Ruth to return to Moab. Orpah tearfully kissed

Naomi good-bye, but Ruth clung to her. Naomi pushed her away but Ruth refused to leave. "Where you go I will go, and where you stay I will stay," she said. "Your people will be my people and your God my God."[12] Ruth wasn't just committing to Naomi, she was pledging her allegiance to God.

The whole town of Bethlehem was stirred when they arrived.[13] Naomi had been gone for ten years, and the townsfolk remembered her, but they didn't immediately recognize her. "Can this be Naomi?"[14] They had to ask because she looked different now. Bitterness will do that, especially if flanked by misery and resentment. Naomi's new identity was reflected in her face, bearing, and attitude.

Naomi announced that she was returning to Israel empty. She forgot—or didn't fully appreciate—Ruth's love, loyalty, and sacrifice. Dear, devoted Ruth! She traveled for days with Naomi, all the way from Moab to Israel. She *clung* to this woman. Ruth loved Naomi through the saddest, hardest season of their lives.

Naomi's heart was broken. Losing a husband and two sons is devastating. Nobody "gets over" grief so deep. It's never easy to say good-bye, and Naomi couldn't quickly or easily walk through her pain. She let it consume her. Bitterness took root and became her identity, smothering whatever seeds might have blossomed.

BODY BLOSSOM—

Change of Identity

Starting a journey with someone never guarantees you'll end together. Planning your life doesn't mean it will unfold the way you expect. Building a nest doesn't make people stay. Every person, experience, and moment we are given is a gift from God. Nobody earns or deserves a gift! Happy relationships, healthy bodies, and good fortunes are moments to be cherished, lightly held, and gracefully released when the season ends.

Sometimes we gain our identity from God's gifts instead of God himself. We fall into the trap of becoming the role—wife, mother, caregiver, organizer—instead of making it one part of our lives. When our identity is rooted in a specific role, we have a hard time releasing it when the season passes. Relationships, family, homes, and even our appearance can become trees in which we build our identities. When the tree falls, we lose ourselves and can't move forward.

What to Do

Name your top five identities. They might be positive: valuable employee, wife, Christian, best friend, marathon runner. Identities can be negative too: victim, nag, stupid, troublemaker, fat girl. Identities can be self-imposed, such as choosing to become a wife or remain a victim. They can also be externally enforced, such as when a supervisor expects you to perform duties not in your job description.

Your identity is the name you call yourself, and names are powerful! How you label yourself directly affects your thoughts, attitudes, choices, friends, and even your health. Think about how your identity affects your behavior, decisions, and your ability to heal from the past. Are you stuck because you can't let go of an old identity? The first step is simply becoming aware of how it affects your thoughts, feelings, and behaviors. Then, start exploring healthy ways to root your identity in Jesus instead.

Flying Back to Mama Bird

Let's revisit Mama Bird in her nest: What if she ignored the lumberjack's warning thuds at the base of her tree? Understandable, for she'd built a comfy home in a healthy tree with lots of shady leaves. Not to mention oodles of bugs and worms to feed her babies! Mama Bird was a *mama*, after all, not a soaring eagle or a trotting turkey. She couldn't just fly or waddle away from her home and start over.

When the lumberjack shook the tree, Mama Bird decided to hold tight to the nest and ignore the new season. When the lumberjack started chopping, Mama Bird buried her head beneath her wings and clutched her babies close. When the tree crashed to the ground, down came Mama Bird, nest, baby birds, and all—flailing in an explosion of bark, branches, and dirt.

Dazed, Mama Bird gathered her babies on the forest floor, nestling amidst broken branches and fallen leaves. She decided to rebuild right there on the ground because she just couldn't leave her familiar surroundings. But then the crows circled, snakes slithered, darkness crept in . . . and Mama Bird realized she had to make a decision. She could stay on the ground and face the known threats, or take a risk and re-nest in a new tree. Shaken and scared, she wished she didn't feel so alone.

But look! A flock of geese was flying overhead, two robins trailing them. If they were flying so free and fearless, perhaps she should test her wings.

Naomi Tries to Fly Solo

They were already on the road to Israel when Naomi changed her mind. Ruth and Orpah had packed up their lives and said good-bye to their loved ones. They'd convinced their families that moving to Israel—enemy territory—was a good idea. They'd prepared food and provisions for the journey. Ruth and Orpah were committed.

But Naomi stopped. And spoke her mind. She told her daughters-in-law to go home because life would be too hard in Israel. Perhaps she was putting their welfare first, knowing it wouldn't be easy for Moabite widows to settle in Bethlehem. Maybe she was protecting herself, not eager to go home with foreigners. It was bad enough she was returning bereaved and defeated . . . but empty *and* flanked by the pagan women her sons married? Risky.

Changing your mind is difficult when you're already heading in one direction. Reversing course is even more serious when your decision affects other people. Nevertheless, Naomi didn't question herself or even apologize for the inconvenience. She spoke her mind firmly. She believed in herself. She didn't allow Orpah's tears or Ruth's disappointment to influence her decision.

Ruth, too, had a mind of her own. She refused to leave Naomi. She was determined to walk into a new life in Israel and build a relationship with God. She believed a fresh season had already begun and she wanted to keep moving forward. Maybe Ruth heard the Lord say, "See, I am doing a new thing! Now it springs up; do you not perceive it? I am making a way in the wilderness and streams in the wasteland."

We'll follow Ruth and Naomi's example as we explore this chapter's final Blossom Tip. We have the freedom to change our minds or stick with the path we chose. God has blessed us with the freedom to think, choose, and recalibrate if necessary.

BRAIN BLOSSOM—
Change Your Mind

Maybe you made a choice that was right for you in the past but doesn't fit you now. The role—or road you're walking—doesn't suit who you are today. You're different. Maybe you learned something new about yourself, someone else, or a situation. You have new information or a fresh insight, and that changes everything.

Or maybe you have no choice but to move into a new season. Like Mama Bird's tree crashing down, you're forced into an unplanned life because of a death, loss, or disappointment. You never expected to deal with that circumstance, emotion, or event. You never wanted or prepared for it to happen, but it did. You can't go back, but now you have a choice: root in the remains or re-nest in a whole new forest.

Everything you experience has been sifted through God's hand. Listen to Him, like a wise Mama Bird heeds a lumberjack.

What to Do

Choose to change your mind about something you've been telling yourself. For example, some women say, "I'll never get over my loss; I can't be happy single. I'm nothing without him." Others say, "It's too late to change my life; I've been working in this job too long. I'm not qualified to do anything else." And still others say, "I don't know God's will for my life, so I won't do anything. I'll keep waiting for a sign."

The more attached you are to your beliefs, the harder it is to change your mind. Be gentle yet firm with yourself. Pay attention to warning signs that it may be time to fly out of the nest. Nurture your growth with compassion and care. Changing direction in life can be difficult, especially when other people are involved. It's even harder when they're unsupportive or critical! However, they are not the source of your strength, identity, or calling. Jesus is. Stay focused.

QUESTIONS *for* JOURNALING *and* DISCUSSION

1. **Nose-to-Nose:** How do you feel about picturing yourself face-to-face with Jesus? Do you have a visual image of God or the Holy Spirit?

2. **Surprise!** When a transition didn't happen as planned, how did you cope? What did you learn about yourself, others, life? How did it change your relationship with God?

3. **Friends:** What has changed in your friendships? How do you make new friends these days?

4. **Change of Identity:** Which identities, positive and negative, have you chosen? If you've outgrown any identities, how can you replace them?

5. **Change Your Mind:** How would changing your mind about something—at work, home, church, or in a group or community—affect other people? What impact does their reaction have on your decision?

What do you think of the Mama Bird parable, or the idea of changing the direction of your life? Come, share your thoughts with me at BlossomTips.com/Naomi.

Growing Forward

Sometimes we're forced to face a new season, and it's hard. It *hurts*. Leaving a familiar home or beloved person is painful— even if we have no choice, even when we actually chose to leave and start over. Take time to rest and reflect. When you're ready, Ruth and I will walk with you into a fresh new chapter.

5

Starting Fresh with Ruth

Even when you faithfully and willingly choose to walk into a new season, you can never be sure what will sprinkle—or storm—into your life. These Blossom Tips, inspired by Ruth's decision to start over in Israel with Naomi, begin with a long, dry season of homesickness in Africa.

Homesick

When I moved to Africa, I expected to eat goat stew and chapati, hear Swahili, see giraffe and gazelle grazing on the roadside, and slosh through torrential rainy seasons. I was even prepared to track lions and tigers on safari! But I wasn't prepared to live amidst giant flying termites with voracious appetites and endless life cycles, baboons breaking in and stealing cookies and cereal from kitchen cupboards, dangerous carjackings and kidnappings at lunch, or fat avocados and mangoes falling off trees with juicy thuds.

I taught middle and high school for three years at Rosslyn Academy, an American school in Nairobi, Kenya. My students—the children of missionaries and expatriates from all over the world—were adept at adapting to new cultures. Many had lived in several countries before they landed in my classroom. Most could drink the tap water because their bodies had developed a tolerance to foreign parasites and bacteria. These kids quickly picked up new languages because their minds were agile, and they felt at home anywhere because they'd been everywhere.

My students also knew how to handle a steady stream of believers from all over the world. Christians came for short- and long-term missions trips, leaving after a week, a month, six months. This was hard on me. I struggled with the constant hellos and good-byes; every person I met took a little piece of my heart home with them when they left.

God planted me in Africa, but I didn't flourish there.

Ruth Leaves Home

When Ruth moved to Israel with Naomi, she left her home, family, and culture. She was starting over as a destitute, childless widow in Israel—a country that regarded her as the enemy. As a Moabite, Ruth was entering foreign territory with unfamiliar customs, rituals, language, and people.

Her only companion was her mother-in-law, Naomi—an empty-handed, brokenhearted widow who would rather be called bitter than pleasant. Naomi couldn't see the blessing of Ruth's love, loyalty, and companionship. She didn't believe in Ruth's vision of a fresh start in Israel, and tried to push her back to Moab. Naomi was returning to Israel in defeat, empty of the promises she and her husband, Elimelek, had left to claim. All she had was Ruth the Moabite daughter-in-law, who was actually a symbol of her son's disobedience to God. Israelites were forbidden to marry their pagan neighbors.

And yet Ruth insisted on going with Naomi. She was determined. Something was calling her, pulling her toward Israel. Love! I believe Ruth had fallen in love with the God Naomi served— even though Naomi wasn't exactly singing His praises at that time. In fact, just the opposite. Naomi announced who was responsible for her problems and misery; she said the Almighty had turned His hand against her[1] and made her life very bitter.[2] Even so, she never stopped believing He was actively working in her life.

Somehow, Ruth must have experienced God's love and power during her ten-year marriage to Mahlon. She wanted to leave the gods and idol worship behind in Moab. Ruth sensed the Lord's love and faithfulness in those dark days and nights, through the trials of leaving her family and immigrating to a foreign country with nothing but hopes and dreams. She knew she was on the right path. Was Ruth homesick and afraid? Probably. Did she keep walking? Yes! Her stamina and steps inspired the first Blossom Tip of this chapter.

SPIRIT BLOSSOM—
The Next Step

Instead of overthinking the next step in your life—whether it's a big leap or a little change—believe God is guiding you. Even if you don't feel a discernible tug or hear a loud shout, trust that He is leading you onward. You can proceed confidently in the direction of your dreams!

As Oswald Chambers writes in *My Utmost for His Highest*,

> When you have a right-standing relationship with God, you have a life of freedom, liberty, and delight; you are God's will. And all of your commonsense decisions are actually His will for you, unless you sense a feeling of restraint brought on by a check in your

spirit. You are free to make decisions in the light of a perfect and delightful friendship with God, knowing that if your decisions are wrong He will lovingly produce that sense of restraint. Once He does, you must stop immediately.[3]

What to Do

Take small steps forward in your life. Look for the open and closed doors that invite you to proceed or warn you to stop. Acknowledge that sometimes a closed door is simply a sign to yield or shift direction. Remember how God led you in the past; reflect on how He guided our sisters in the Bible. Learn how He speaks to your fellow Christians today.

Often, the first step is research or information gathering. Explore the possibilities, discover opportunities. Are you bored and unfulfilled? Try a different volunteer or work role, join a new group, go on a missions trip. Are you struggling with fear, anxiety, or paralysis? Get support. Take a commonsense risk, and remember that God isn't trying to trick or confuse you. You don't need to find His "perfect plan," for *you are God's will.* Stay connected to Him in daily prayer and Bible reflection. Walk simply and steadily, one step at a time.

Open Doors in Africa

Three closed doors had to swing open before I could move to Africa. First, I needed to find a job at a Christian school that actually paid its teachers (as opposed to teachers raising their own money, like many missionaries do). So I prayed. "Heavenly Father, if it's your will that I teach in Africa, please give me a paying position. I can't picture myself raising money. I'm not rooted in a home church or a spiritual community, I have nobody to lean on. Please help me financially."

Second, I was still studying to be a teacher. I was finishing the last three courses of my education degree at the University of Alberta and needed special permission from three professors. I would have to take my final exams early to be in Africa for the first day of school. Two instructors immediately granted permission; the third refused. He said I'd miss too much coursework. Plus, he had an ethical problem with a new teacher not completing her full course load before teaching. Eventually, after I prayed and petitioned and persevered, he permitted.

Third, my only option in Africa—Rosslyn Academy—refused to hire me. That door slammed shut! Their policy was to hire teachers with at least one year of experience. Plus, their positions were filled for the upcoming year. Woe was me for a month, until out of the blue they requested a phone interview. The eighth-grade teacher they had hired changed her mind about taking the position, leaving an unexpected opening.

And so to Africa I moved.

Ruth Sees an Open Door

After moving to Israel, Ruth and Naomi struggled to survive. Fortunately, barley harvest had begun, and the fields were thick with grain. Ruth asked for permission to glean, which involved collecting grain scattered along the field's edge left by the workers. Gleaning, it seems to me, would have been humbling and socially stigmatizing. In Leviticus 23:22, the Lord commanded farmers to leave extra grain at the edges of the field for the poor and the foreigners. People who needed to glean were struggling to survive. Perhaps gleaning felt like asking for spare change or applying for public assistance today.

As it happened, Ruth found herself gleaning on the edge of a barley field owned by a man called Boaz.[4] Coincidentally, Boaz was an honorable man who—luckily—turned out to be one of Naomi's relatives.[5] Fortunately, God required family to take care of each other in hard times. When Ruth randomly ended up in Boaz's field, Naomi thanked God for His provision (she knew luck had nothing to do with it).[6] Happily, they'd met a kinsman- or guardian-redeemer who could—and eventually did—rescue them from poverty and restore their lives.[7]

Hold on, wait a minute, back up! Look at all the lucky breaks, coincidences, and happy accidents in the previous paragraph. Those weren't random occurrences at all! On the contrary, God had a grand plan for Ruth and Boaz in the barley field. God was working behind the scenes the whole time, showing His love and attention through those "acts of fate."

Ruth and Boaz became King David's great-grandparents.[8] Ruth is named in Jesus' own family lineage.[9] The echoes of God's work in that barley field reverberate in our lives today. And they're the heartbeat of our next Blossom Tip.

HEART BLOSSOM—

Open Doors

Our Creator surprises us by opening some doors and closing others. He dazzles us with brilliant moves and unpredictable twists and turns. Sometimes, sadly, He disturbs and dismays us with hardship and loss. But don't despair! God uses tragedies to lay the foundation for triumphs—even when we can't see how, why, or where. His endings lead to fresh beginnings; life springs from death.

God invites us to partner with Him. The only way to build a strong, healthy relationship with Him (or anyone) is to walk together through the highs and lows, risks and rewards, good and bad. God wants you to be an active participant and co-creator in your own life. You mustn't sit and wait for opportunities to knock and doors to open. No, that's too easy. And easy isn't interesting. Easy is, in fact, a yawn.

What to Do

Pay attention to the "coincidences" and "accidents" in your life, for they could be seeds planted by God. He might swing open a door and thrust you into a new life, uprooting and replanting your future. Or He might open the door a crack and let a little light shine in, perhaps giving you a vague idea or even a firm offer. Sometimes God introduces you to new people who share interesting options or suggestions. Or you stumble across opportunities that seem unlikely or even impossible at first.

Don't give up, even when you're facing a closed or half-open door. Go slow, reminding yourself that faith is being sure of what you can't see. Lean on half-open doors with curiosity. For example, I applied for a teaching job at a school with a policy of only hiring teachers with experience. That was a half-open door because I had the right education but no experience. I leaned on the door, and God opened it.

Who knows what might happen? Boldly knock on doors and be willing to consider anything. Remember that behind closed doors you find fresh new worlds.

All Together Now

I was always proud of being strong and independent because I did everything alone: survived foster homes, set myself up in an apartment when I was seventeen, finished high school, made my own money, bought a car, paid my bills, earned university degrees, moved to Africa. I congratulated myself for not needing anyone, not even God. I went my own way because I didn't want Him to tell me what to do. I wasn't bitter, nor did I think God brought misfortune on me. I just didn't think He cared.

Writing this chapter helped me see how God shows His love and power through relationships—even formal and professional ones. For example, look how many people were involved in my move to Africa! Finding the teaching job required the internet, which was created by people I'll never meet. Getting my education degree required professors, university administration, and schools to train and mentor me. Working in Africa involved Rosslyn's administration, support staff, parents, and students. I can't even count all the people involved in my physical relocation to Africa.

I was never alone; I just *thought* I was. Like Naomi, who thought she had nobody when she actually had a daughter-in-law worth seven sons.[10] Naomi didn't realize how much she needed Ruth—or that Ruth needed her too. Without Ruth, Naomi would have remained empty, poor, and bitter. Without Naomi, Ruth wouldn't have met God, left Moab, or found Boaz. Ruth and Naomi were interdependent.

Ruth and Naomi Leaning In

Ruth helped Naomi set up and settle into their new home. Naomi taught Ruth how to live in Israel: who to talk to, what to say, and how to interact in Hebrew culture. They shared the practical struggles of daily life as well as their fears and anxieties about the future.

It was Ruth's idea to glean, but she asked Naomi first.[11] Working in the barley fields as a Moabite woman made Ruth a target for verbal harassment, physical assault, even rape. But they had no choice, so off to work Ruth went. After a hot day picking grain from morning to night, Ruth brought home a sack full of barley. She also had leftovers from the lunch Boaz gave her.[12] Without Ruth's hard work, resourcefulness, and likability (Boaz didn't offer lunch to *all* his field hands), Naomi would have starved.

Without Naomi's knowledge of Hebrew customs and culture, Ruth wouldn't have gleaned. Nor would she have risked reaching out to Boaz. She didn't know Boaz from Adam. Not only did Naomi know who he was, she was *related* to him. He was her kinsman-redeemer, a relative who by Old Testament law was required to help them out of poverty.[13] Naomi guided Ruth through the doors God opened.

Leaning on each other's strengths and bridging their weaknesses didn't just change Ruth's and Naomi's lives—it changed the course of history. Our next Blossom Tip illustrates the power of interdependent relationships.

SOUL BLOSSOM—
Interdependence

Consider the difference between independence, dependence, and interdependence. Independence means you're completely separate and self-governed—and it's rare. Truly independent women wouldn't use the city's electricity or sewage system, shop at stores, or work with others. Independent people are hermits living alone on remote islands, detached and inaccessible.

Dependence means needing someone or something to live. Babies are dependent. People who can't move, swallow, or breathe without a machine are dependent. In most relationships, total dependence is unhealthy and limiting. For instance, consider a woman who relies solely on her husband for survival, or her children for meaning in life. When she loses the person, she loses everything. Not good.

Interdependence, as Ruth and Naomi demonstrate, is ideal because it involves mutually beneficial relationships. Strengths and resources are shared. So are needs and weaknesses.

What to Do

Use a visual technique to see how independence, dependence, and interdependence already exist in your life. Create a Venn diagram by drawing three overlapping circles, about the size of soup cans. Write "Me" in the left circle, "Others" in the right, and "God" in the top circle. The middle overlapping part of the three circles is the sweet spot! It's where you, others, and God are all interconnected.

Now, consider your past decisions. Which circle are they in? For instance, my move to Africa was in the sweet spot because everything aligned: me, God, and others. Before that, my decision to live alone at seventeen was solely in the "Me" circle.

Do you depend too much on others and not enough on God? If your past decisions were based mostly on others' opinions, for example, then you may be overly dependent. Learn how to depend on God and build healthy interdependent relationships with people.

Sweating It Out

When my application to teach at Rosslyn Academy was first rejected, I was a little relieved. Relocating to Africa would be a hassle! I had a cat, car, roommates. Not to mention doubts: What if committing to a three-year contract in an unpredictable third-world country as a single woman was a mistake? At the time, Kenya was politically, socially, and economically unstable. Nairobi was one of the most dangerous cities in the world, home to the highest rates of violent crime, property theft, carjackings, and vigilante justice for lawbreakers. It was a risky place to live.

But then came regret. I couldn't shake my yearning to go, explore, take a leap of faith. I kept searching for teaching jobs, but I couldn't find a Christian school that offered a paid position. I couldn't afford to volunteer and didn't want to raise my own financial support. The longer the African door stayed closed, the more I wanted it to open. Time was running out; positions for the upcoming school year were quickly being filled, both overseas and locally. I needed to find a job.

I lived with the school's rejection for a month, wondering the whole time if teaching missionaries' kids overseas was really what I wanted (it was), continuing to search for jobs in Africa and Europe (unsuccessfully), and praying that God would open the right door (*please*).

Then the phone rang. The eighth-grade teacher Rosslyn had hired changed her mind, and I was up for an interview. Immediately I knew I was moving to Africa. I'd had a month to sweat it out and I used that time to pray and reflect. Without that season of waiting, I always would have wondered if going to Africa was a mistake.

Ruth Sweats It Out

Ruth spent her days, dawn till dusk, picking grain in the fields. She gleaned for two or three months, sweating in the hot, dry fields until harvest season ended. She also sweat it out one night near a pile of grain. The night that changed her life, the night she risked everything by offering herself to Boaz, as described in the third chapter of the book of Ruth. That night, she crept into the dark field after the workers had eaten and drunk their fill. She uncovered Boaz's feet and lay there while he slept.

Talk about sweating it out! Ruth was a Moabite gleaner—a foreigner, an enemy of Israel, a poor widow—proposing marriage to a wealthy, well-respected older man. She didn't know if Boaz would be insulted, disgusted, or even abusive. What if a worker saw her before Boaz did? Sweaty patience for Ruth, but not for God. His plan was for Boaz to wake up and be pleasantly surprised to discover Ruth. And that's exactly what happened.

There was only one hitch: another man. Boaz wasn't Naomi's closest kinsman-redeemer. Naomi had another relative who was first in line to marry Ruth, and Boaz had to give him the chance to do so. Naomi and Ruth had no choice but to wait and see what would happen next.

Waiting for God's plans to unfold isn't easy, even when we're leaning into Him. We need to stay close so He can wipe the sweat and tears away. Our next Blossom Tip describes my 80 percent rule, but I love knowing that God is available 100 percent of the time.

BODY BLOSSOM—
The 80/20 Rule

I'm committed to running (often uphill and backward, which is sweaty work!) or doing yoga 80 percent of the week. I exercise *most* days, allowing myself to have "exercise free" days about 20 percent of the time. Same with food: I'm committed to eating fruit, veggies, and nutritious food 80 percent of the time. This allows me to dig into cheeseburgers, fries, and hot fudge sundaes 20 percent of the time.

My 80/20 Rule gives me freedom, which changes my attitude toward exercise and eating. I don't feel constricted or deprived. I feel like I'm making a conscious, life-giving, healthy choice to do my body and brain good. This isn't a diet and exercise plan, it's a way of life that helps me stay healthy and happy. I feel lighter and more energetic overall, especially on the 80 percent days.

What to Do

Apply the 80/20 Rule to three parts of your life. Go beyond eating and exercising! For example, maybe you often stay up late at night and feel exhausted in the morning. Commit to going to bed early most nights (80 percent of the time), and allowing yourself a late night sometimes (20 percent). Or maybe you always considered taking a ballet or rowing class but didn't feel fit enough. Commit to showing up 80 percent of the time or attending 80 percent of the class, and giving yourself freedom to be a "no show" 20 percent of the time.

In your spiritual life, commit to trusting God with your whole heart, mind, and soul *at least* 80 percent of the time. How about even 95 or 100 percent? You are His child, which means you can trust Him with every detail of your life *all* the time. You may believe this intellectually, but still experience bouts of anxiety and fear. This is normal! Trusting God wholeheartedly can be a leap of faith for even the most faithful Christian. Right now, simply commit to trusting Him with more—and more important—aspects of your life.

More Valuable than I Realized

Living in Kenya was both the best and worst time of my whole life. It was the hardest thing I've ever done and the richest season I ever experienced. Teaching a class of boisterous thirteen-year-olds in an unpredictable and sometimes violent country was difficult—even though the students were well-behaved, bright, and motivated. I felt overwhelmed and exhausted most of the time. I made so many mistakes. I wasn't the teacher I wanted to be.

But despite my shortcomings, God was at work. Recently, I received this email:

Dear Miss Pawlik,

My name is Nick, I was one of your students at Rosslyn! Long story short, my wife and I found some old "keepsakes" from Africa. One was the Language Arts journal I wrote in while I was in your class! It was awesome! We spent the morning reading old entries and laughing about how sassy and ridiculous I was!! Of note, I couldn't stop writing about airplanes and becoming a pilot. It turns out that I DID become a pilot—I'm flying the MV-22 Osprey for the Marine Corps and completed two deployments. You taught me to write better—and that opened up numerous doors, including the US Naval Academy and living my childhood dream as a pilot! Thank you for investing in my life!!!

I felt like I was a mess in Africa, yet God used me. I showed up with my fragile little offering, and He created something of value that still echoes today.

Ruth's Value

Ruth married Boaz, who was Naomi's guardian-redeemer. He was a family member, obligated to help a relative in serious difficulty. Boaz was a good man, the hero who rescued Ruth and Naomi from a life of poverty and childlessness. He gave them a fresh start in life.

However, let's not forget that Boaz also benefited from his union with Ruth! He even told her how valuable she was. He called Ruth a noble, worthy, virtuous woman of excellence.[14] He commended her for gathering grain for two or three months, for not approaching other, younger men. Ruth was a smart, loyal, hardworking, loving woman who clung to God. She wasn't afraid to sweat in the fields, present herself to the right man, and take life-threatening leaps of faith. Ruth was an incredible woman of great value to Naomi, Boaz, her community, and us today.

Did Ruth recognize how valuable she was, I wonder, or was she distracted by her mistakes and regrets? Often we overlook our strengths and contributions. We focus on our weaknesses and failures, belittling or forgetting our contributions to this world and God's kingdom. We may never know how important our "little" lives are, especially when we're doing mundane chores at home or stressful projects at work.

Ruth never knew there would be a book named after her in the Holy Bible. She didn't know she'd be in Jesus' own lineage and that God would change history through her personality, gifts, and hard work. She never knew how valuable she was . . . but God did.

As we reach the end of this chapter, let's pause and celebrate how far we've come! Seeds have been planted; many are already starting to take root. Our last Blossom Tip gives us time to stop, breathe, and honor the gift of ourselves.

BRAIN BLOSSOM—
Write Back

When you don't know your own value, you believe lies. You're hobbled or even paralyzed by your mistakes, regrets, and failures. You let people belittle, dishonor, or even abuse you. You forget that God made you the way you are *on purpose* and that your life is unfolding according to His plan. You have an important place in this world, and we need you to step up with dignity, delight, and confidence! We need you to turn away from doubt, fear, and insecurity. We need you to see yourself as a valuable gift from God. Give yourself permission to be who you are without guilt or apology.

Honor God by finding and developing your strengths. Notice what sets you apart from others. God wired you differently from other people; maybe you're silly or serious, artsy or athletic, creative or cerebral. Value yourself so you can bless others with your gifts.

What to Do

My favorite group activity is called "Write Back." In this exercise, everybody tapes a piece of full-size paper (at least 8 1/2 by 11) to their back. Everyone takes turns writing something on each person's back—a trait they admire or value—in a few words. Sometimes whole paragraphs are written! Anonymous comments are best because they encourage free expression. Sometimes chains of people writing on each other's backs are formed, creating a great photo opportunity for the group.

The most powerful benefit is how people feel when they're *writing* on others' backs. The emotional effect of noticing, appreciating, and sharing positive qualities about others is amazing. At the end, after everyone has written on each person's back, everyone gets to read their own paper. It's delightful and often illuminating to see what others see and appreciate in us.

QUESTIONS *for* JOURNALING *and* DISCUSSION

1. **The Next Step:** Do you spend more time searching for God's perfect will than taking small steps forward? What do you think about the idea that your commonsense decisions are God's will for your life?

2. **Open Doors:** What door has God slammed shut in your life? Where do you see opportunities for a change in direction or attitude?

3. **Interdependence:** Are you dependent on someone or something (e.g., social approval, your appearance, money)? What healthy interdependent relationships do you enjoy?

4. **The 80/20 Rule:** What is one unhealthy habit you're planning to change? How does it feel to commit to something—such as a healthy eating or lifestyle habit—80 percent of the time?

5. **Write Back:** In what community might you lead this back-writing exercise? Consider your family, small group, or even workplace. Two people are all you need! If you participated in this activity, what surprised you?

Our last Blossom Tip in this chapter is a group activity. If you aren't reading this book with others, go to BlossomTips.com/Ruth and share the top three things you like most about yourself. I'd love to hear from you!

Growing Forward

We're turning over a new leaf and floating into the New Testament. Mary and Martha knew Jesus' love of gardens and heard His parables about sowing seeds, reaping harvests, picking grain. He was even mistaken for a gardener once! But alas, I'm getting ahead of myself. Let's take it one season at a time.

6

Growing Roots with Martha and Mary

Jesus doesn't always heal what we *want* to be healed. Sometimes He heals what *needs* to be healed. The Blossom Tips in this chapter grew from seeds healed and unhealed in my life, as well as several thorny issues faced by our biblical sisters Mary and Martha.

Not Like the Others

I sat cross-legged on the top bunk in my new bedroom. I could touch the ceiling if I stretched; glow-in-the-dark stars and planets were scattered hither and yon. Maybe the kid before me was scared of the dark.

The social worker opened the door and poked her head in, asking me to join her and the foster parents for a snack, to get to know each other a little before she left. My new foster mom was talking about the nearby school, and my sister had the grown-ups laughing with her knock-knock jokes. The other kids would be home soon, the social worker said.

Our first foster home. My mom was in the hospital because of schizophrenia, and I had a couple thousand questions. How long would she be gone? What if this foster home was bad, like ones I'd read about? Who were the other kids and why were they here? Would my sister and I attend the same school? When my mom got better, where would we live?

I also had questions about me. Why couldn't I just be normal and chatty, like everyone else? I could hear my younger sister laughing in the living room while I sat frozen in the bedroom. If only I could be more like her. She always told me, "Don't be so sensitive!" And I'd try. I tried hard to be easygoing and fun, but I couldn't be like my sister.

Our Biblical Sisters

Martha is known for being practical and preoccupied with preparing the comforts of home and food for her houseguests. Her sister, Mary, sat learning at Jesus' feet—unusual and even scandalous for women in those days. She opened her heart and absorbed every moment with Him.

These sisters chose to spend their time and energy differently because they had unique personalities, abilities, and gifts. They expressed their love for Jesus in different ways. The problem? Martha wanted Mary to care about the things she, Martha, cared about. For example, she wanted Mary to serve but didn't ask for help. Perhaps she already knew the response: "I'll be there soon," or "Yes, the minute Jesus leaves." Martha knew Mary wouldn't—or couldn't—change.

So Martha approached the only person who could change Mary. "Lord, don't you care that my sister has left me to do the work by myself? Tell her to help me!"[1]

But Jesus didn't tell Mary to be more like her sister. He didn't urge her to conform to Martha's or anyone else's expectations. Instead, He accepted Mary for who she was. "Martha, Martha, you are worried and upset about many things, but few things are needed—or indeed, only one. Mary has chosen what is better, and it will not be taken away from her."[2]

Jesus also accepted *Martha* for who she was, telling her the truth and letting her decide for herself. Jesus loved both Martha and Mary unconditionally. Not only does He give us the same gift of love and acceptance, He encourages us to recklessly re-gift! Our first Blossom Tip shows us how.

SPIRIT BLOSSOM—

Regifting

Your traits, abilities, proclivities, and passions are important to Jesus—and to the world. Whether you're raising kids or running a factory, your presence and personality matter. Maybe you feel like an outsider at home or work because your quirks aren't understood or appreciated. Maybe you're different in big or little ways, and you feel pressured to conform. Maybe you don't believe you have any gifts or talents at all.

Jesus knows you. He sees your eccentricities and foibles, and He loves you more because of them! That's what makes you *you*. He accepts your crooked smile and zany thoughts, your penchant for collecting ceramic chickens and cool crosses. All He asks is for you to show up and sit at His feet. No need to make profound observations or ask brilliant questions. Simply receive His gifts. Then, consider giving Him a gift of your own.

What to Do

Accept Jesus' gift of unconditional acceptance. You needn't strive, push, work harder, or be better, because He loves you just the way you are. Bask in His warmth. Now, rewrap this gift of unconditional love and give it back to Him.

How do you regift to God? By accepting and loving Him for who He is—just like He does you. God is holy yet available, complex yet kind, mysterious yet loving. He has allowed a variety of experiences into your life: joy and pain, beauty and tragedy, sunshine and storms. Give Him the gift of surrender and faith by choosing to release your doubts, fears, and confusion. Talk through your questions and struggles, then trust Him.

Regift God's love by embracing both what you have and what you've lost. Delight in who you are and who you aren't. Give Jesus the gift of unconditional acceptance and trust.

Twin Sisters

My mom had an identical twin sister. They were Moreen and Doreen! They grew up wearing the same clothes, hairstyles, makeup. People couldn't tell them apart, even when they were in their fifties. My aunt didn't have schizophrenia like my mom, but she battled mental illness and addictions all her life. She died at age fifty-eight from a terrible combination of Parkinson's and ALS (Amyotrophic Lateral Sclerosis, or Lou Gehrig's disease). It was a progressive and painful death: Her body slowly twisted up and wasted away; her throat and vocal cords withered and shriveled. She was kept alive with feeding tubes and pain medication. Her heart finally stopped beating.

I never knew what to say when I visited her in hospice—she used to be my wild, colorful, reckless Auntie Doreen! Always off on adventures, dying her hair different shades of blond, flirting

112

with men of all ages, starting her own businesses, selling real estate. Now she couldn't talk. She could only groan and blink. Her brain seemed alert when I visited, her eyes following me as I roamed her room, picking up random objects and trying to find something to say.

After seeing her, I'd call my sister. She refused to visit the hospice and eventually stopped taking my calls. She said she wanted to remember our aunt the way she was, wearing red cowboy boots and leopard-print skirts. My sister refused to face the pain of disease and death.

I didn't blame her. Nobody races toward death. Not even Jesus.

If Only, Jesus

Jesus loved Mary and Martha, yet He let them experience terrible loss and grief. He allowed their younger brother, Lazarus, to get sick and die. Jesus eventually showed up, but not in time to prevent death. "Lord, if you had been here, my brother would not have died," said Martha.[3]

A little later, Mary said the same thing: "Lord, if you had been here, my brother would not have died."[4] At first, I found it incredible that Mary and Martha repeated those exact words to Jesus. Then I realized they probably said the same thing—"If only Jesus were here"—to each other repeatedly while Lazarus was sick.

"If only Jesus were here . . ." said Martha as she fed and cared for her dying brother. "If only Jesus were here . . ." said Mary as she petitioned God and prayed the psalms. Both sisters watched the door, expecting Jesus to show up and save Lazarus.

Because they knew Jesus loved them, they believed He would heal Lazarus. After all, when you love someone, you give them everything they want, right? You say yes to every request, right?

Wrong. Jesus said no to people all the time. Even people He loved.

It hurts when God says no. Disease and death are dreadful. And it doesn't always help to believe God has something "bigger and better" planned because the anguish of watching a loved one die can't be erased. Neither can the grief.

The only way to escape suffering is to follow Mary and Martha through the pain, all the way to Jesus. It also helps to look for sprouts and blossoms in the valleys.

HEART BLOSSOM—
Don't You Care?

Martha had an advantage when she asked Jesus to solve her family problems—which she never hesitated to do. She was lucky; she could talk to Him face-to-face and receive immediate feedback. "Lord, don't you care that my sister has left me to do the work by myself? Tell her to help me!" Jesus didn't always acquiesce to Martha's requests, but at least she could tell Him *what* she wanted ("Make Mary work!" "Heal Lazarus!") and *when* she wanted Him to do it (now!).

Wait a minute . . . if Martha can do it, so can we! We know Jesus hears us, and He actually wants us to talk to Him. It doesn't matter what we say or how we say it, as long as we show up. So let's do it. Let's tell Him what's on our minds and hearts. And let's take it a step further by telling Him how to fix our problems, people, and pain—no matter how silly or outrageous our solutions seem.

What to Do

Finish this sentence: "Jesus, don't you care that _____? Tell her/him to _____!" Imagine Jesus doesn't know your problems or pain. Pretend He doesn't know what's burning in the kitchen or breaking your heart.

I'll go first: "Jesus, don't you care that my sister won't talk to me or my mom? Tell her to love us, to come back to us!" Writing the truth is painful because it forces me to face what hurts most. But writing also helps because it loosens the pain, gives it air and space, lets me breathe. Jesus flows through the dirt clumps; His presence relaxes me. I let go. I accept and surrender. I feel lighter.

Try it. Write this sentence: "Jesus, don't you care that _____? Tell her/him to _____!" Be honest. Nobody will read what you wrote. Express what you need and want. Then, take a deep breath. Open your heart and let Jesus heal.

Unexpected Healing

When I read my childhood diaries, I remember how hard it was to live with a schizophrenic mother. The hospitalizations, shock treatments, and antipsychotic medications didn't heal her. Sometimes they helped, but she didn't like the uncomfortable, often painful side effects. She also didn't like feeling "spaced out," like she was moving through cotton. So she'd stop taking her pills, and the hallucinations and nervous breakdowns would return. This cycle lasted for decades, destroying the fabric of her mind and body.

As my mom spiraled downward, her physical, verbal, and emotional attacks increased. She was unpredictable, unstable, scary. I prayed she'd get better, but God never healed her. I wasn't angry, nor did I stop believing in Him. I just didn't think He cared. I thought I didn't matter to Him or anyone.

God never cured my mom's schizophrenia, but He healed my relationship with her. Now I call her at her group home every

GROWING FORWARD WHEN YOU CAN'T GO BACK

Sunday; she has no other contact with family. It's an adventure, talking to an eighty-year-old schizophrenic woman who is going deaf but refuses to wear hearing aids, can't focus on one topic for more than a few minutes, and isn't allowed to talk about her environment because everyone can hear every word.

Sometimes Jesus doesn't heal what we *want* to be healed, but what *needs* to be healed. I wanted Him to heal my mom's brain. Instead, He healed my heart.

Lazarus Lives

Before Jesus brought Lazarus back to life, He wept.[5] His heart broke when Mary fell at His feet, sobbing because her brother had died. "When Jesus saw her weeping, and the Jews who had come along with her also weeping, He was deeply moved in spirit and troubled."[6] Jesus *saw* Mary, He *heard* them crying, and He *felt* their pain. He didn't cause Lazarus' death, but He walked with them through their pain and grief.

Our Creator has ultimate power over our experiences—and He has sent illness and natural disasters to specific people, as recorded in Scripture. However, horrible diseases also happen because of biology, genetics, and our fallen world. Here's how one rabbi handles the grief and pain: "I try to get people to see God not as the source of the illness, the accident, the tragedy," says Harold Kushner, author of *When Bad Things Happen to Good People*, "but as the source of their resilience. . . . God is with you in this."[7]

We move through the pain not by avoiding or blaming God, but by turning to Him for strength, comfort, and healing.

When Mary and Martha turned to Jesus, He didn't lecture them about strength or trusting God's plan. He simply wept, knowing this world isn't what God envisioned. Then Jesus raised Lazarus from the dead to glorify God and strengthen their faith. "See, I am doing a new thing!" says the Lord. "Now it springs up; do you not perceive it? I am making a way in the wilderness and streams in the wasteland."[8]

If Martha had a lot of chores to do on an average day, imagine her workload after that! Their home was already crammed with mourners offering comfort, support, respect. Afterward, it would have erupted with even more relatives, friends, neighbors, perhaps even curious passersby. Lazarus would have needed cleaning, feeding, counseling, hugs. Lives were changed forever.

Their songs of praise would have been spontaneous and uncontrollable. Sometimes we, too, erupt in bursts of worship, but mostly our days are ordinary. Guess what? I discovered a Blossom Tip to help us sing hallelujah in even the dreariest seasons.

SOUL BLOSSOM—

Hallelujah Anyway

What if you praised God for who He is—no matter what was or wasn't healed in your life? Saying "Hallelujah anyway" means loving God because He is holy, powerful, and awesome. Singing "Hallelujah anyway" means letting His will be done simply because He's *God*. He flung the stars across the sky and scattered starfish in the deepest parts of the sea. He knows every nook and cranny of every mountain on earth. This is the God who knows and created *you*.

What can you give your powerful, awesome, holy God? Your worship and praise. Set aside your pain and problems for fifteen minutes. They'll be there later. Put them down and pick up your conductor's baton. Yes, your baton! It's time to conduct the choir.

What to Do

Cue the music! Dig out your favorite songs. Maybe you love hymns such as "How Great Thou Art" or "Come Thou Fount of Every Blessing." Or maybe you're keen on carols like "Angels We Have Heard on High" or "O Holy Night." Maybe your spirits soar with musicals and movie soundtracks, such as *Mamma Mia!* or *The Sound of Music.*

Pick up your baton (or knitting needle, or chopstick) and stand quietly for a moment. Square your shoulders, plant your feet. Clear your throat and lift your chin. Raise your arms and hold the baton loosely. You're the conductor! Hit "Play," close your eyes, and lose yourself in the drums, guitars, saxophones, violins, tambourines, flutes, and cymbals. Cue the musicians by waving your arms, marching your legs, swaying your body, bopping up and down. Worship God by getting lost in the songs and sounds He created! Lose yourself in the joy of singing "Hallelujah anyway."

A Miracle Cure

Before Jesus healed Lazarus, He was "once more deeply moved."[9] Jesus didn't weep briefly with Mary, then bring Lazarus back with a solemn nod of His head. Rather, Jesus first experienced *waves* of grief. He responded from His heart and spirit to the mourners' pain. He didn't suppress His tears. Jesus' grief—like ours—doesn't hit once and disappear. Loss might pummel us repeatedly for a while, then become a wispy shadow that we always carry. That's the bad news. The good news is that loss doesn't have to destroy our spirits. In fact, loss can purify and magnify our joy, peace, and faith if we keep our eyes fixed on Jesus.

Look what He did next! Jesus didn't go into the tomb; He called Lazarus to come out. Martha was right: It must have stunk in there.[10] After all, Lazarus had been dead for four days. We have no record of his experience; perhaps an angel appeared in the tomb, helped him sit up, then told him to keep his lips zipped about life after death.

"Take off the grave clothes and let him go," Jesus said.[11] I love it! Take off your shackles and chains, my friend, for you are free. Mary and Martha rejoiced.

But guess what? Lazarus probably got sick again, as we humans do. He eventually died. So did Mary and Martha. Jesus didn't come to shield us from earthly disease and death. He never promised to heal all our infirmities and answer our prayers the way we want. No, Jesus does *better* than that! He offers an endless wellspring of joy, peace, and power. He helps us rise above the saddest, lowest seasons of life. And this, my friend, is what our next Blossom Tip is all about: Getting over the bumps in the road.

BODY BLOSSOM—

Bumpy

I have two incurable diseases: bunions and ulcerative colitis. My bunion ("Bumpy") is, unfortunately, alive and well. Bold and chatty. Thankfully he doesn't holler and howl like he did when he first grew on me! Now Bumpy just constantly babbles in the background. I've had my other disease—colitis—for two decades, and it's taken me almost that long to learn how to keep it in remission. After years of experimenting with medications, diets, and lifestyle changes, I finally found what works for me.

Perhaps you're dealing with your own version of Bumpy: chronic pain, disease, depression, addictions, eating disorders, heart problems, eye conditions, joint issues. Maybe you're recovering from a treatment such as knee surgery or chemotherapy. Maybe you're coping with a terminal illness. Since we all have (or will have) Bumpys that accompany us everywhere, we might as well make friends with them.

What to Do

Experiment with different ways to take care of your Bumpy. Try different treatments, therapies, and healthcare providers until you find a solution. Explore your options and keep detailed records of the remedy you tried, who prescribed it, when, and what resulted. Remember that your body, brain, and soul are interdependent! If you don't get enough sleep, nutritious food, or heart-pumping exercise, you'll feel slow and low. That won't help Bumpy.

Make peace with the possibility that God may never heal your affliction. Or perhaps He'll heal you in unexpected ways. Give your Bumpy to Jesus, and pray your heart's desires. Lean on Him for strength, energy, and healing. Let His will be done in your body. You, Bumpy, and Jesus are doing life together.

Buckets of Energy

At 4 a.m. every day, God wakes me up with a Bucket of Energy. It sloshes over with joy, energy, and inspiration—I can barely carry it! But as the sun travels across the sky, my energy leaks out into work, people, chores. By 7 p.m. my bucket is empty.

I recently realized I have the power to *choose* how to spend my energy. I used to relive painful memories, revisit my shame and regret, ruminate on my mistakes and weaknesses. Not anymore! I don't have to spend my energy on meaningless activities, conversations, or conflicts. I don't have to waste my time on movies, books, or websites that pull me down. I can stop trying to control other people's thoughts and choices.

One of my *She Blossoms* readers, Molly, helped me see this. She spent a decade of energy on her marriage, hoping her husband would change, praying for a miracle. "I desperately wanted a good relationship," she wrote. "I couldn't let go. I often thought of Paul's miraculous conversion on the road to Damascus. I prayed God would do the same for my husband."[12]

God does restore relationships, heal afflictions, and grant miracles! But the very definition of "miracle" means the chances are miniscule. Miracles are extraordinary, supernatural, *astonishing*. Further, Jesus didn't perform miracles to make people happy. He performed miracles to glorify God and reveal himself as the Messiah.

Pray for miracles with a childlike heart: open, curious, trusting. Pick up your God-given Bucket of Energy and pour yourself into His plans for your life.

Martha's Bucket of Hospitality

Martha poured her energy into serving houseguests, ensuring bellies were fed, and keeping bodies warm and comfortable. Her ministry was practical, and probably delicious. Her sister, Mary, spent her time sitting at Jesus' feet and absorbing His teaching. These women had different interests and abilities; their use of time and energy revealed who they were and what they thought important.

Jesus related to them differently, according to their personalities and perspectives. When Mary and Martha said the same thing, that Lazarus wouldn't have died if Jesus had been there, He responded two different ways. Martha had also added, "But

I know that even now God will give you whatever you ask."[13] She was calm and analytical, and Jesus met her where she was. They talked theology. Later, when Mary wept at Jesus' feet, He matched her energy and emotions. He met Mary in grief and wept with her.

Because Mary and Martha were distinct individuals, Jesus responded to them in unique ways. He loved them equally but treated them differently.

I love that Jesus, too, had a Bucket of Energy. In a separate encounter with a different woman He said, "Someone touched me; I know that power has gone out from me."[14] He knew when His energy was leaking out. He knew when He had to withdraw and refill by retreating in solitude to spend time with the Father.

Imagine that. As a man, Jesus had access to the Holy Spirit's power and energy, which was endlessly available and directly applicable to His daily life. And so do we! In this chapter's last Blossom Tip, we'll learn how to fill our buckets and keep them topped up.

BRAIN BLOSSOM—
Bucket of Energy

Writing this book—especially my childhood bits—took a surprising amount of emotional, spiritual, and physical energy. It also took time and effort to research, plan, write, and edit each chapter. This taught me the importance of not wasting a drop of energy! I had to keep reminding myself not to get distracted by unproductive pastimes (social media, kitty cat videos), negative thoughts (who cares about my past, anyway?), and destructive emotions (doubt, discouragement).

I also realized I have the power to *choose* how to spend my time and energy. Changing my old ways of thinking and acting was a struggle at first, for both me and other people. I had to be firm with family and friends, allowing them to be disappointed when I chose not to spend time watching movies or visiting. I learned how to say no to things that didn't serve my calling and to let people respond as they wish.

What to Do

Picture your Bucket of Energy. How big is it and what fills it up? How long does it last? Do you take time to refill it, or are you constantly running on empty? Think about the people and activities you pour your time and energy into. Are you serving God's call on your life? If you don't know what God wants you to do, then start there. Use your energy to explore, experiment, discover!

Start by noticing the small daily choices you make. Ask yourself if this is *really* how you want to spend your time and energy. God gave you the gift of life—and, yes, sometimes it gets boring, tedious, even painful. Instead of allowing monotony or grief to deplete your energy, choose how you will live each day. Decide what seeds you will sow. Tend your garden by pouring your energy into activities and thoughts that are true, right, and worthy. Your fruit will multiply in ways you never thought possible, and so will your energy.

QUESTIONS *for* JOURNALING *and* DISCUSSION

1. **Regifting:** What would it feel like to fully accept—and even rejoice in—*everything* God allows into your life? How

can you surrender to everything from spilled milk to hospice visits?

2. **Don't You Care?** In what ways do you feel God has let you down or disappointed you? How do you cope when it seems like Jesus doesn't hear or care about you or your loved ones?

3. **Hallelujah Anyway:** How does it feel to put on headphones, turn up your favorite music, and conduct the musicians? If you don't know, try it today!

4. **Bumpy:** Describe how a health condition is affecting your life. What do you think about giving your affliction or disease a name, personality, and reason for existing?

5. **Bucket of Energy:** What do you spend the majority of your time and energy doing? Thinking? Remembering? If you were ninety-nine years old, what advice would you give yourself today?

Your thoughts and stories about anything in this chapter (or book!) are welcome on BlossomTips.com/MarthaMary.

Growing Forward

When we first meet her, Hannah is carrying an empty Bucket of Energy. Did our biblical sister stumble across a secret wellspring of life? Let's see how she revived her heart—and how we can too.

7

Reviving Your Heart
with Hannah

Your heart changes everything! These Blossom Tips, inspired by Hannah's broken heart, will help you overcome barriers to wholehearted living. My favorite tip in this chapter is walking down Memory Lane—and it all started in Las Vegas.

The Pit of Despair

"Nothing good has happened since my husband left me three years ago," writes Ellen, a *She Blossoms* reader. "All I have is bitterness and anger. I feel lost and alone, like I can't cope without him. I'll never forgive him. I feel like I'll never find happiness or meet someone else at this stage in my life. Next year I turn fifty-five. I'm so desperate, I just don't know what to do. I am absolutely broken. A complete mess. I have nowhere to turn."[1]

To make matters worse, her husband's divorce lawyer petitioned to decrease his alimony payments, sell the family home, and split the profits. The judge ruled in his favor. Ellen was forced to pack up the house they'd lived in for over twenty-five years and move to low-rent accommodations. The judge suggested she go back to school and find a fulfilling career path. "He said I should look for ways to support myself that also give me purpose. Ha! Not in this lifetime."

Ellen is angry, bitter, and sad about how her life turned out. And she has every right to grieve! It's not fair or right that her husband left after thirty years of marriage. It's scary to be forced to sell a home in midlife and face the future alone.

There's nothing good about being thrust into an unexpected and painful new season of life, feeling like you have nothing left and nobody to lean on . . . or is there?

Hannah Collapses

Instead of a haven, Hannah's home was a hive of pain, mockery, and disunity. Worse, as we read in 1 Samuel 1, she couldn't get pregnant after years of trying. Childlessness wasn't just heartbreaking for our biblical sisters, it was also socially stigmatizing. Infertility was a sign of dishonor, worthlessness, and future economic instability. Hebrew women had nothing to fall back on—no education, meaningful work outside the home, or even the possibility of pursuing other life dreams or goals.

Even worse, Hannah had to share her home with Peninnah, who was the second wife of her husband, Elkanah. Peninnah had her own sons and daughters, and often goaded and provoked Hannah to tears.[2] Perhaps Peninnah was jealous and hurt because Elkanah gave Hannah double portions of sacrificial meat. He wanted to make Hannah happy, not understanding that his gifts couldn't fill the emptiness in her heart.

"Hannah, why are you weeping?" Elkanah asked. "Why don't you eat? Why are you downhearted? Don't I mean more to you than ten sons?"[3] Hannah reassured her husband that she loved him, but he couldn't fill the emptiness in her spirit and soul.

She was so depressed she couldn't eat or stop crying. Nobody understood and nothing could comfort her. It was this suffering—Peninnah's taunts, Elkanah's inability to understand, and her own tormented heart—that drove Hannah to God. If her relationships were happy and her life perfect, she wouldn't have collapsed at the Lord's feet. And her heart wouldn't have changed.

Hannah poured herself out to God, trusting that her cries would rise above the noisy din of grief, confusion, and fear. Her focus and faith inspired the first Blossom Tip in this chapter. Can we find God even in the rowdy crowds of places like Las Vegas?

SPIRIT BLOSSOM—

Vegas

Ding ding ding! Jangling slot machines, noisy jackpot payouts, the clanging of coins crashing into metal pails—Las Vegas must be the loudest place on earth. I was disappointed when we first arrived; our hotel was two blocks from the main strip. But when we left Vegas four days later, those two blocks were my path of peace. Deep, quiet, and rich. God met me there, soothing my soul after the main strip's hustle and bustle.

Now, looking back, I believe God was on the main Vegas strip too. He can be found amidst the clanging slot machines and crowded poker tables. He's just harder to hear in the clamor. The world jumps, screams, and competes for our time, attention, and energy. God waits quietly in the noise and pain, turmoils and troubles. He's in the divorces, disappointments, and loneliness. If we look, we'll see Him through the smoke and mirrors.

What to Do

Invite Jesus into the chaos of your life. No need to wait for a women's retreat, the perfect worship service, or a sun-soaked Sunday afternoon. Silence and solitude are wonderful places to hear His voice, but they're not always available. Practice meeting God in the clamor, noise, and distractions of daily life. Tune your heart so you hear Him above, below, and through the roar. If you can sense the Holy Spirit in the hubbub, you'll see Him anywhere and everywhere.

I practice finding God in distracting church services. I used to be annoyed when the worship team didn't play "the best" songs, the pastor didn't preach "the right" sermon, babies cried, men sneezed, and women snored. But now those distractions remind me that God isn't just found in stillness. He's alive and waiting for us in life's daily noise, distractions, and chaos.

A Lucky Escape

Shirley's divorce was similar to Ellen's—except for the ending. "My husband left me after thirty-one years," she writes. "He was terrible and nasty through the divorce. He's totally different than the man I thought I knew the years we were married. I try to have as little contact with him as possible, but I hear news from friends."[4]

Her ex-husband lived with his girlfriend until she kicked him out. He moved in with his daughter (Shirley's stepdaughter) and her family. His business fell apart and his two mini-strokes caused other health issues. He has a new girlfriend whose son is running from the police. This is causing problems for him, his daughter, and his grandchildren.

"As for me, I quite enjoy living on my own," Shirley writes. "I planted the nicest garden I ever had, and started decorating areas of my house I never liked. A lovely stray cat moved in. I always wanted a cat, but my husband was allergic. I go on holidays with friends. So, as much as I never planned this part of my life—I'm fifty-seven—it's turning out pretty good. I look at my ex-husband and don't recognize the man he's become. Sometimes I think I had a lucky escape."

Shirley's advice to women facing divorce? "You'll get through this and learn your strengths. I'm so sorry we were betrayed, but we have to forgive and let them go. Don't let them take more of you than they already have."

Hannah Finds a New Life

Hannah collapsed in the Lord's temple. Her heart was set on getting pregnant, but she didn't just want to have a baby. Her whole identity was rooted in her ability to conceive. Her family, culture, and yearning for a child blinded her to everything else. Getting pregnant wasn't just one aspect of who she was; it was everything. It was all she cared about.

When Hannah couldn't have the one thing she wanted, her heart broke. And then along came Peninnah to stomp on the pieces. Unnecessary and cruel, yes. But Peninnah's provocation wouldn't have been so painful if Hannah's heart had been fixed on God's love, power, and strength.

What healed Hannah's heart? God. But He didn't just miraculously make her whole and drop a baby in her lap. Hannah healed by taking action. She went to the Lord's house and sought His presence. She realized she'd never be happy unless she stopped making everything—pregnancy, babies, family—about *her*. Instead of desperately yearning for God's blessings, she had to set her heart on God himself.

And she did. Hannah pushed pregnancy off the throne of her heart and put God there instead. And He gave her the desires of her heart! But it wasn't quick or painless; her transformation took time, energy, and willingness. "In her deep anguish, Hannah prayed to the Lord, weeping bitterly."[5] She didn't instantly conceive a baby after setting her heart on God, but she immediately experienced healing, peace, and joy. The physical blessings came later.

Hannah flourished, and so can we. Here's how a Basket of Blossoms can nurture peace and joy in our minds, bodies, and hearts.

HEART BLOSSOM—
Basket of Blossoms

Whatever your heart is set on has control over you. For example, if your heart is set on having a baby but you can't conceive, you'll be devastated. If your heart is set on finding your soul mate or having a perfect family, you'll be destroyed if your relationships don't go as planned. Whatever sits on the throne of your heart—marriage, work, money, appearance—controls your life.

It's normal and healthy to be sad when life disappoints or hurts you. Losing someone or something you love is a terrible experience, and you must grieve. However, if you're stuck in depression or pain, perhaps your heart was set on something that couldn't live up to your expectations.

Everything in life will eventually let you down. People leave or die. Homes get sold or destroyed. Money and jobs come and go. Our health declines, abilities weaken, and beauty fades. Our hearts will be crushed if they're set on God's gifts instead of on God himself.

What to Do

Look at the people around you; who needs encouragement and hope? *Everyone.* Create a "Basket of Blossoms" for someone you know—a co-worker, relative, friend, neighbor. Find a small basket, flowerpot, glass jar, or any container. The more unusual, the better! Cut fourteen pieces of paper into squares or rectangles that can be rolled into small scrolls. Use markers or colored pencils to write specific messages of joy, hope, and encouragement. Tie the scrolls with a ribbon or string.

The more personal your messages, the better. Share your memories, such as, "Remember when we _____? That was so funny/scary/crazy!" Or "I'll never forget the time you _____." Or perhaps, "Every time I see/hear/smell _____ I think of the time _____." Tell your friend to read a message every day. Her heart will blossom with the love of God, and so will yours.

On My Throne Sat Books

Our hearts aren't always set on relationships or families. For instance, my heart was set on being a writer; my first book was a city guide called *Unveiling Vancouver.* I pitched it to a dozen publishers and received a book contract! But the deal fell through because I moved to a different province in Canada. My heart was crushed, my self-esteem shattered.

My second book was *Traveling Teens, Rocky Roads*, but it didn't get published. My third was *See Jane Soar*, a book of life lessons from famous women. Amelia Earhart! Wangari Maathai! Coco Chanel! A New York City literary agent offered to represent me, but he couldn't sell it to the first few publishers he tried so he dropped me as a client. Alas, another season of sadness and disappointment. I abandoned all hope of getting published, deciding that writing blog posts was good enough for me.

But it wasn't good enough for God.

Ten years later, on a California road trip with my husband and dogs, I found myself at a Christian writer's conference. I didn't plan on meeting a literary agent, polishing my book proposal writing skills, or writing *Growing Forward When You Can't Go Back*. Nor did I plan on signing a contract with a publishing house a couple of months later.

And yet, here we are.

When getting published stopped being about *me*—my dreams, goals, identity—my books and blogs blossomed. I happily signed a contract to write this book, but I would have just as happily continued blogging. My heart changed, and that changed everything.

Hannah's Prayers

Her heart was shattered because she couldn't get pregnant. At the Lord's house, Hannah wept bitterly.[6] She poured out her soul and prayed in anguish *for a long time*. Deep pain requires deep healing. Deep healing is a process—a season—that takes time, energy, and acceptance.

Hannah prayed aloud and quietly in her heart, her lips moving silently and her emotions spilling over. Her prayers were personal, reflecting her personality, emotions, and relationship with God. Maybe she swayed, her arms held high, her head raised. Or maybe she collapsed in a sodden heap on the ground. However it appeared, Hannah's encounter with God was so intense that Eli the priest thought she was drunk.[7]

Her life changed because she sought God instead of dwelling in her pain, grief, and disappointment. God was there, waiting and listening. But He didn't immediately drop a positive pregnancy stick in her lap. He didn't promise she'd be blessed with many sons and daughters, or that Peninnah would stop being mean. And yet, Hannah's heart lifted. She didn't feel sad or discouraged anymore! She praised God even though she didn't know what her future held.

"Then she went her way and ate something, and her face was no longer downcast. Early the next morning they arose and worshiped before the Lord and then went back to their home at Ramah."[8] Even though God promised her nothing, Hannah felt happy. Why? Because her heart was set on God himself, not the gifts He gave.

Hannah's heart was healed by her cries. Crying is a healthy and good way to connect with God, but we can also find Him in more creative endeavors.

SOUL BLOSSOM—

Praying in Color

As a child, you drew and colored with abandon—maybe even outside the lines. You expressed your heart and creativity! Let's take a page from childhood and pray in color. Drawing and coloring your prayers can help you get beyond the barriers that block authentic heart-to-heart communication. Praying in color isn't about creating masterpieces; it's about expressing your feelings without worrying about saying the right words.

In her book *Praying in Color: Drawing a New Path to God*, Sybil MacBeth describes how to doodle and color prayers. Your drawings can be abstract shapes or specific objects. You can draw whimsical words and play with bubble letters. Maybe you'll doodle hearts and circles with different verses or prayers inside. God created crayons, paints, paper, shapes, textures, and tones—use His handicrafts to talk to Him! He'll love your art if it expresses your heart.

What to Do

Open your Blossom Journal, or find a piece of paper. Grab a pencil or markers. Colored pencils and crayons are great; watercolor, acrylic, or oil paints are even more exciting! Bring whatever you have to the table. God requires your willingness and participation, not artistic talent or perfection. He just wants you to express the bright and dark parts of your heart.

You might create glorious orange sunrises or black blobs of grief. Maybe pink happy faces or droopy flowers. Maybe you draw circles with people's names inside or boxes of problems you need to give to God. Feel stuck? Sketch a big flower with petals in the middle of the page. Write the word "Blossom" in the center of the flower. On each petal write words like *joy, peace, freedom*—whatever comes to mind. What are you grateful for? Hoping for? What do you want Jesus to do for and in you?

Don't worry about drawing perfectly or beautifully. Focus on finding and expressing the desires of your heart. Pray in color.

Remind God of His Promises

"God loves to be reminded of His promises," said my pastor one Sunday morning. At first I didn't understand this. Why would God want to be reminded of His promises? He's not like a parent hoping his child forgot the promise of Disneyland on spring break: "But you *promised*, Dad! You *said* we'd go!"

"Why do you think God likes to be reminded of His promises?" I asked my husband on the way home from church. Bruce figured that when we remember what God promised, we show we were actually listening when He spoke. And remembering shows we value God's words, that His biblical and personal promises are important to us. The longer we remember the Lord's words and actions—and the more often we talk about His promises with Him and others—the more meaningful they are.

More important, God tells us to remember His words. Throughout Scripture He exhorts us to write His teaching on our hearts,[9] to fix them in our minds,[10] to bind them to our hands,[11] and to write them on our foreheads[12] so we see them constantly.

One of my favorite passages to remember is Isaiah 43:19: "See, I am doing a new thing! Now it springs up; do you not perceive it? I am making a way in the wilderness and streams in the wasteland."

I love to remember my experiences of God *with* God. I talk to Jesus about how He took care of me through the dark valleys and dry spells of my life. I remind God how the Holy Spirit protected me from dangers, toils, and snares. I remember the blessings He has given me. I remember by writing in my journal, meditating at night when I can't sleep, and walking down memory lane with Jesus.

God Remembered Hannah

"Lord Almighty," said Hannah, "if you will only look on your servant's misery and remember me, and not forget your servant but give her a son, then I will give him to the Lord for all the days of his life."[13]

Hannah dedicated her first child, Samuel, to God. This meant she wouldn't have her son at home after he was weaned or when he grew up. She wouldn't enjoy the social, economic, or personal benefits of having the boy she waited years to conceive. This vow shows how profoundly her heart and life changed! It wasn't about Hannah anymore; it was about God.

God had told Abraham He would save the world through a Hebrew boy. Every Hebrew mother knew her son could be used by God as part of His plan for salvation. But that would require letting her son go. Hannah's vow to dedicate Samuel was her way of aligning herself with the Lord's work and participating in His ministry. She wanted to be part of His hope, healing, and restoration.[14]

Hannah set her heart on God, and He changed her motivation. He placed new desires in her heart and He granted those desires. Hannah learned the joy of submitting to His will, praising Him for who He is, and relinquishing control of how her life "should" be.

Her son Samuel became the prophet who anointed Saul as the first king of the Israelites. Hannah's heart healed, and her life changed history. And all because she remembered God and asked Him to remember her. Her experience inspired our next

Blossom Tip, which is one of my favorite ways to spend time with God.

BODY BLOSSOM—

Memory Lane

"Remember when I moved to Africa, God?" I asked, wandering through the forest with my dogs. "I was so excited and scared. Getting on the plane for a three-flight, two-day journey, not knowing who was going to meet me at Kenyatta Airport, starting my first job at an American school, teaching missionaries' kids—wild! Do you remember how guilty I felt about leaving my sister, Jesus? That was hard. So was teaching. I felt so alone and insecure. Remember those starry nights when I walked around the track at school? Sky so dark, stars so bright. What an awesome experience, God! Thank you."

When you recall specific memories—both positive and negative—with Jesus and people who shared the experience, you strengthen your connection with them. This is powerful in your relationships with family, friends, co-workers, and even neighbors. Remembering reinforces your shared history and increases feelings of attachment.

What to Do

Pick a few meaningful moments in your life, a mixture of good and bad. Tell Jesus those stories while you're walking, washing dishes, standing in line at the store. Ask Him what He remembers, and open your mind to ideas and inspiration. If you feel like crying, take time to be sad. If you feel like singing and dancing, get up and wiggle! If you're hurt and confused, tell God. Collapse at His feet. Sometimes it's good to remember the bad.

You might also reminisce about events that occurred before your birth. In church last Sunday, I thought of David dancing in Jerusalem. "Remember how David worshiped joyfully and freely, filled with the Spirit?" I said to God. "The king of Israel leapt amongst the maidservants and musicians in the street! And then he got in trouble with Michal later, remember? Oh, Jesus, David really was a man after your own heart."

Transforming Your Heart

There's one problem with setting our hearts on God: It doesn't come naturally. Scripture memorization helps, and so does meditating on verses like Proverbs 3:5: "Trust in the Lord with all your heart and lean not on your own understanding." Maybe you even remember Paul's words in Colossians 3 about setting your heart and mind on things above. But actually *doing* it— focusing on God and releasing the worries, fears, and struggles of daily life—is different.

After their husbands left, both Ellen and Shirley wrestled with forgiveness and acceptance. Their hearts were set on their plans for the future. Forgiving their husbands for betraying them after decades of love and marriage was a long process. To make matters worse, Ellen and Shirley weren't just disappointed by their husbands. They felt let down by the Lord too. "God, why did you let this happen?" they asked. "I thought you loved me."

Disappointment and grief can become barriers to God. Ego is another barrier. My heart and self-image, for instance, was set on my books getting published. When I was rejected by literary agents and editors, I struggled with shame, failure, and unworthiness. Sharing my writing with people was difficult, but rejection was devastating because it confirmed my worst fear: I wasn't good enough. My heart was set on my worldly perspective, not God's grace and love.

Our biblical sister Hannah knew the pain of unworthiness, insecurity, and grief. She, too, had to overcome barriers of doubt and anxiety so she could move forward in her life.

Hannah Stood in Glory

"So in the course of time Hannah became pregnant and gave birth to a son. She named him Samuel, saying, 'Because I asked the Lord for him.'"[15] Note the words *in the course of time*. This means Hannah didn't get pregnant immediately. Another biblical translation says Hannah conceived before the year was out, which means she might have spent twelve months trying to get pregnant. A year is a long time to wait, hope, and persevere.

Meanwhile, Hannah was living with Peninnah and her children. To stay faithful to God, she had to forgive Peninnah for tormenting her so cruelly. Hannah couldn't allow bitterness or resentment to take root and grow in her heart. She had to find ways to forgive Peninnah and live in peace, as much as it depended on her. How did she do it? Maybe she meditated about her experience in God's house, praising Him for who He is and remembering her vow. Maybe she remembered God in her heart, thoughts, and prayers. In due time, the Lord blessed Hannah—and the world—with the prophet Samuel.

When we align our heart with God, He gives us our heart's desires. He *delights* in giving us good things the way parents love surprising their children with gifts, even when it's not Christmas! But a fulfilling, rich life of faith isn't found only in God's gifts in seasons of joy and peace. Rather, a deep relationship involves changing our heart so that no matter how stormy or scary life gets, we always find our way home.

This chapter's final Blossom Tip reveals the most common barriers to setting our hearts on God, and offers solutions for overcoming obstacles.

BRAIN BLOSSOM—
Under the "B"

"B" is for barriers to be overcome before our hearts can change. How many of these obstacles apply to you?

10 Possible Barriers:

1. Setting your heart on external accomplishments (e.g., writing a book, having a baby).
2. Allowing a relationship or marriage to become the center of your life.
3. Letting sorrow, grief, or loss take root and grow in your heart.
4. Blaming others for your past, pain, or paralysis.
5. Refusing to pursue a relationship with God.
6. Expecting an immediate solution—or a miracle—from God.
7. Trying to solve the wrong problem.
8. Being too proud to admit your heart is cold, distracted, or broken.
9. Not being honest with yourself about what your heart is *really* set on.
10. Refusing to ask for what you need and want.

Take time to think and reflect. Open your mind to receive the Holy Spirit's wisdom and guidance.

What to Do

Copy each barrier into your journal, noting your feelings. Answer these questions:

- Is this true for me? What evidence do I have?
- How does this affect my life and relationships?
- How does God fit in?

Go beyond your first responses. Work through the obstacles that stand out to you, and leave the rest for now.

This can be a daily, weekly, or monthly practice, not a "one time only" exercise. It could become part of your Sabbath, a different way to connect with God. Pay attention to the idols that keep crawling onto the throne of your heart. Your relationship with Jesus is growing—even if you can't see or feel it right now. Keep nurturing these seeds, and you will blossom.

QUESTIONS *for* JOURNALING *and* DISCUSSION

1. **Vegas:** How have you experienced God in times of turmoil, confusion, or chaos? What does it feel like to find stillness in the storm?

2. **Basket of Blossoms:** If you have nobody to share a Basket of Blossoms with, recall a loved one. What memories would you include in their basket?

3. **Praying in Color:** How do you feel about praying by drawing, painting, or sketching? What is the most creative way you've prayed?

4. **Memory Lane:** When are you most likely to share memories with loved ones? Do you talk about good times, bad times, or both?

5. **Under the "B":** What people, places, or things keep creeping onto the throne of your heart? How do you feel about a regular practice of setting your heart on God?

I'd love to hear the Blossom Tips that revive your heart, spirit, and soul. Come, share with me on BlossomTips.com/Hannah.

Growing Forward

Our next biblical sister had her queenly heart set on one thing: saving the Jews from complete annihilation. She quickly learned how to flourish into a new season of life, blossoming from the quiet Hadassah to the regal Queen Esther.

8

Renewing Your Purpose with Esther

Warning: The contents of this chapter may disturb you, as they did me. Fear not! We'll hasten through the dark shadows and enter the palace of our biblical sister Queen Esther. She blossomed after facing her secrets and fears. So shall we.

It Almost Happened to Me

One dark night, when I was eighteen and living alone, I woke to see a man kneeling at the foot of my bed. *Impossible!* I thought, squinting. *Must be a pile of blankets.*

He reached over to pet my cat. Blankets don't move! Time to scream. *What if no sound comes out, like in a nightmare?*

I screamed anyway.

What if nobody hears me?

He thrust his hand down my throat. I tasted cigarette smoke. *I'll stop screaming, I can't breathe, I promise I'll stop, I'll stop!*

He pulled his hand out. We wrestled. "Please don't do this. I'm a virgin."

"Sure you are," he said. I needed another plan. My clock radio! I fumbled for it and blasted the volume. *Maybe a neighbor will come knocking. But what if I can't answer?*

He reached for the plug and slid off the bed. *Yes!* I scrambled away, my eyes fixed on the door. *Run!* He grabbed my ankle. "Oh, baby, come back." *No!*

I raced upstairs to my landlord, who was watching TV. "I heard a scream," he said, "but I figured it was the movie." We called 9-1-1 and went downstairs to my apartment.

My kitchen knife was on the floor by my bed. He'd set it down to kneel, pet my cat, watch me sleep. *What if I had woken when he was carrying the knife? What then?*

I was running from God in that season of my life, but He hovered anyway.

It Happened to Her

Before she became Queen Esther, she was a Jewish orphan girl called Hadassah. We don't know what happened to her parents, how old she was when she lost them, or if she was with them when they died. We don't know if she had brothers or sisters. Hadassah was raised by her older cousin Mordecai; they were exiled Jews living in the land of Persia.

The king of Persia—Xerxes—banished Queen Vashti for refusing to parade her beauty before his guests at a wine-soaked feast that had started seven days earlier.[1] The king needed a new queen; hundreds of girls were brought to the palace to audition. Our biblical sister Hadassah was included, but nobody knew she was Jewish. She spent a year in the harem undergoing beauty rituals, royal training, and a complete identity change. She was being prepared for one night and one goal: to meet and please the king. To be the chosen queen.[2]

Hadassah was transformed into Esther, and she was more beautiful and agreeable than all the other harem girls and concubines. Esther pleased Xerxes and was crowned queen of Persia, which filled her life with unforeseen, unexpected responsibilities and stress. If she felt sad about not having her own home or family, she grieved quietly.

Our biblical sister Esther was facing an unknown future as a Jewish girl hiding her true identity in a Persian kingdom. If she was anxious or afraid, she hid it well. I don't know if Esther fretted or fussed, but I do know how Jesus responds when I get scared. Which brings us to our first Blossom Tip . . .

SPIRIT BLOSSOM—

What Then?

Even now—thirty years after that guy broke into my apartment in the middle of the night—sometimes I feel afraid when I'm home alone. Especially if I hear weird noises. That's when I play the "What Then?" game with Jesus. He asks questions and I answer.

It goes something like this:

"A guy breaks in," Jesus says. "What then?"

"I react instinctively and fight like before, I guess."

"What then?" asks Jesus.

"I survive. I know you're here. We'll get through it, like we do."

"What then?" asks Jesus.

"I call 9-1-1. Maybe he'll be arrested. I don't know."

"What then?" asks Jesus.

"I'll get help, maybe counseling, who knows. We'll figure it out when it happens—*if* it happens."

"What then?" asks Jesus.

"Will you stop asking so many questions, Jesus?! Our Father is here, and has gone ahead of us. Let's go to sleep!" (*sound of snoring in peace*)

What to Do

Write down The Thing that scares or worries you. Then hear Jesus ask, "What then?" Write whatever pops into your head. Again, Jesus asks "What then?" Keep answering Him, even if you say "I don't know" repeatedly. Because that's the point: *We don't know.* But He does!

You'll see two things:

1. There's no use worrying about the past, present, or future. Fretting wastes your time and energy. Walk through your worries once with Jesus, if you must. Then leave them with Him.

2. You can and will survive. God sifts everything through His loving, powerful hands before it reaches you. You also have unlimited access to the strength, wisdom, and guidance of the Holy Spirit. Not only will you survive, you'll find unexpected blessings in the aftermath. God knows what's coming. He has prepared the way. Take a deep breath and trust Him to lead you through.

My Secrets

Some women aren't comfortable talking about their experiences with sexual abuse or rape, for various reasons. I never had a problem sharing my experience of attempted rape. In fact, I found it easier to talk about than my other ordeals. My childhood secrets felt more embarrassing and stigmatizing, and I worked hard to hide them. Being "illegitimate" was a source of shame when I was growing up. I was born out of wedlock to a single schizophrenic mom who broke her front tooth by gnawing on a frozen bun. Her new witchy look was one more secret to add to my growing pile. We moved constantly, sometimes sleeping on the street, living on welfare, eating in soup kitchens. The worst, however, was the names she called me.

Lots of secrets, nobody to tell. Now I understand why I always struggled with worthlessness, shame, and inferiority. And I realize how much energy it took to hide my secrets.

How did I heal? Many small ways, but mostly by finding the balance between actively building a relationship with God and quietly receiving healing from the Holy Spirit. I experienced regular growth spurts, too, such as the unforgettable morning I listened to a sermon on two little words: "Our Father." Not the whole Lord's Prayer, just powerful insight into the precious, delightful, deep love of *our Father*. My identity changed—but not overnight. It was a gradual process of healing, with unexpected bursts of new growth and fresh blossoms.

I also discovered how hard Satan works to burden us with secrets, shame, and guilt. The devil wants us to hide and huddle in the dark.

Esther's Secret

Hadassah found herself not just living in a world of unfamiliar rituals and customs, but reigning over it. Imagine that! Our little Jewish orphan, placed in a Persian kingdom by God. As Queen Esther, she lived in a palace filled with gold and silver sofas. She walked on mosaic pavements made of mother-of-pearl and expensive stones. She trailed her fingers along marble walls and sipped out of golden goblets.

But it wasn't Esther's *home*. None of the people, traditions, clothes, furnishings, or food were hers. Not a shadow of her past identity and name remained. She was hiding her background, traditions, and family. She had to keep her real name—Hadassah, given by her mom and dad—a secret. She couldn't follow the Jewish laws or customs; everything in her new life went against her upbringing and religion. She lived a double life, unable to share who she was, where she came from, what she thought. Home wasn't a place to let her hair down and be herself. Esther was playing a role and hiding her true identity. She had to stay tightly buttoned up all the time.

She didn't choose this season, but she adapted like a queen. She rose to every occasion and met every challenge even though she didn't know her purpose or future. All Esther could do was take one royal step at a time. The one thing she knew for sure? She had to keep her secrets.

We know something Esther didn't (or perhaps she did!). Secrets will destroy us if we keep them locked up inside. Letting them out will set us free. Our next Blossom Tip shows us how to share in healthy ways.

HEART BLOSSOM—
Your Secrets

What are your secrets? Big or little, they affect your health and happiness—and not in good ways! Secrets have a negative impact on your relationships, forcing you to hide who you are and what you know, saw, or experienced. Secrets take up emotional and mental energy because they must be constantly monitored. They pop up without warning at the worst times and in unexpected ways.

Secrets have surprisingly negative physical effects. Research shows that secret-keepers are more likely to suffer from headaches, nausea, and back pain. Secrets weigh people down and tire them out. In one study, people with secrets found basic chores, such as carrying groceries, more physically burdensome. Secret-keepers have lower motivation, well-being, and stamina.[3]

You may think your secrets are worse than other people's, but the truth is we're all huddled in the same cave. Someone just needs to turn the light on.

What to Do

Recall a secret. Maybe it's something you did, or something done to you. Secrets can be mistakes, accidents, failures, unhealthy choices, unspoken words, unfulfilled promises, unmet dreams, unanswered prayers.

Say your secret aloud or whisper it softly. Don't pressure yourself to tell anyone unless you're ready. Express your secret, perhaps by talking, writing, sketching, painting. If you need forgiveness, ask for it. If you need healing or counseling, find ways to get it. Take responsibility for your mental and emotional health.

Forgive yourself. Sometimes secrets carry so much guilt and shame that forgiveness feels impossible! It's hard to let go of failures and shortcomings—especially if you feel you deserve to be punished. However, torturing and refusing to forgive yourself is a sin because it separates you from Jesus. If you sought forgiveness through Him, you're now clean before God. Stand tall and let the past fade away. You are His child, thoroughly loved and accepted.

A Surprise Confession

Remember the guy who broke into my apartment and tried to rape me? Well, he confessed to the police a year and a half later. This means he spent *eighteen months* reliving the break-in and attempting to move on with his life. He wanted to forget but he couldn't. Maybe he confided in someone who advised him to confess to the police. Maybe he heard a woman describe what it's like to experience or witness a sexual assault. Maybe he watched a violent crime drama on television.

For some reason, he could no longer bear the weight of his secret.

The police asked me to identify him; he pled guilty and was sentenced to two years less a day. Had he not confessed, he never would have been caught! Something kept reminding him of his crime, gnawing on his soul, eating at his heart like rats chewing through wires until the house goes up in flames. See how dangerous it is to keep a secret? Even for rapists and hardened criminals.

I was barely eighteen when he broke into my apartment. I'd emancipated myself from God because I wanted to be free and independent (but I often snuck in a quick prayer before falling asleep). My relationship with God wasn't miraculously restored after the guy broke into my apartment, or even after he confessed. I knew God was protecting me the whole time, but I refused to give up my freedom. Maybe deep down I thought God would wait for me, and I'm humbled and amazed that He did.

God at Work

Meanwhile, back at the palace, Esther was still carrying her secrets. She was the only Jewish woman for miles and she didn't have a life outside the palace. If she had a relationship with

God, she kept it secret. Maybe she remembered her Hebrew ancestors who wandered the wilderness and yearned for home.

Then "coincidences" started happening. These events actually started occurring much earlier, but Esther didn't notice because she was busy becoming the queen of Persia. And that was the first coincidence: Esther was a teachable, smart, strong Jewish woman in a powerful position. She wasn't there by accident. Another lucky break was Mordecai overhearing a plot to kill King Xerxes. He told Esther, who told Xerxes, who appreciated the warning.[4] A third coincidence was Mordecai's refusal to bow to Haman, Xerxes' official. Haman was so angry he ordered the extermination of the entire Jewish race.[5]

When Mordecai instructed Esther to beg Xerxes to reverse the edict and save her people, Esther hesitated. And for good reason! "All the king's officials and the people of the royal provinces know that for any man or woman who approaches the king in the inner court without being summoned the king has but one law: that they be put to death."[6]

Mordecai replied, "If you remain silent at this time, relief and deliverance will arise for the Jews from another place. . . . And who knows but that you have come to your royal position for such a time as this?"[7]

We'll see how Esther overcame her fear. But first let's behold God's awesomeness! This Blossom Tip reveals His creativity and imagination, and will quickly lift your heart and spirit.

SOUL BLOSSOM—

God's Secrets

During my last visit to Israel, I was enchanted by the exotic fish, sharks, stingrays, and coral at the Eilat Underwater Observatory

Marine Park. I admired lemon-yellow fish with bright rainbow streaks, their long, wavy turquoise fins trailing behind them. I marveled at tangled ivory coral that breathed air bubbles, copper sea creatures with crimson hair, electric green eels that twirled and whirled and swirled. The marine names were delightful: Flowerhorn, Tompot Blenny, Goliath Tigerfish, Decorated Warbonnet, Dwarf Clown Frogfish.

God invented breathtaking colors, characteristics, shapes, and sizes of deep sea fish and marine life for . . . what? He didn't create the vibrant hues, patterns, textures, and traits of different creatures, plants, and coral in the deep sea for our pleasure. We rarely see them! They live miles below sea level; their lives and relationships are mysteries to us. I believe God designed them for the pure joy and delight of creating marvelous works of living, breathing art.

What to Do

Go on a Treasure Hunt for God's Secrets. A quick, easy way to discover sea creatures is to search the internet for exotic ocean fish. If you get seasick, find pictures of unusual land animals. Look for echidnas, binturongs, kakapos. Search for variations of common animals such as dogs, horses, insects, or birds. You'll be astounded at the variety of even the most common rodents.

Find pictures of amazing land formations. Look for fairy chimneys, karsts, fumaroles, snow caves. Search for natural wonders such as waterfalls, volcanoes, jungles, deserts. Don't forget the sun, moon, stars, and galaxies!

Everything in nature points to God. Take time to explore, examine, and simply behold His creation. Meditate on the works of His hands, the endless depth of His imagination. Let your heart overflow with awe and wonder. This natural way to absorb God's beauty has the power to heal your heart and spirit.

Trust and Prepare

God's world is beautiful but heartbreaking. I discovered this Arabic proverb soon after the attempted rape: "Trust in God, but tie up your camel." Not owning a camel, I created my own version: "Trust God, but lock your doors. And get a dog."

The home invasion left a bittersweet taste in my mouth. I was disheartened at how terrifying the world can be and felt vulnerable in my own home, where I was supposed to be safe. I was bewildered because I had never engaged in "risky" behavior. I never stayed out late, partied, or even dated. I waitressed at a *pancake house* and went to school every day.

But, oh, the sweet realization that if I wasn't safe at home, I wasn't safe anywhere. So, I figured, I could go anywhere! And I did. I hitchhiked through Europe twice before I was twenty-one, once by myself. I went on long solo road trips in Canada. I didn't want to live alone, so I moved in with a trustworthy male roommate, a cheerful New Zealander called Dean.

The world is risky, but the threat isn't in our location. We can be safe in war zones, or in danger at home. Getting hurt is unavoidable, and God will give us what we need to heal. He hovers, making us safe *everywhere*. But we must do our part by trusting like children, tying up our camels like good stewards, and preparing like smart, brave queens.

How Esther Prepared

Esther underwent a year of physical, mental, and social training before she became queen. Persia was the richest, most powerful country in the world at that time, and King Xerxes was a proud man. The queen had to be perfect. Hence, a yearlong stint of beauty treatments with scented oils, rich ointments, and fragrant perfumes.[8] The harem girls learned the royal rules of etiquette, image, fashion, and jewels.

Esther was beautiful, but so were the others. What set her apart was her likability, agreeability, and cooperation. She listened to Hegai, the king's eunuch who was in charge of the harem. He gave her special food, seven personal maids, and the best place in the palace.[9]

After she was made queen, it wasn't her beauty that saved the Jews. Esther had to be smart and strategic because she was battling Haman, who already had the king's ear. She needed a solid plan.

Esther organized and prepared:[10]

- Three days of fasting for herself, her attendants, Mordecai, and the Jews.
- Two delicious banquets to soften and sweeten King Xerxes.
- A strategy to stop Haman's extermination plan.
- A public confession that she was Jewish.
- Her verbal and social skills to approach the throne.
- Her face, body, hair, and royal garments to please King Xerxes.
- A logical argument that appealed to Xerxes' ego, honor, and reputation.

Esther didn't bat her eyelashes and ask King Xerxes to pretty-please let the poor Jews live. Rather, she used every resource God gave her. She prepared—and executed—a strategy. And she was victorious.

Fasting was one strategy Esther used to prepare for a terrifying task. Her experience inspired the following Blossom Tip for growing forward.

BODY BLOSSOM—

Fast Times

The New Testament doesn't command us to fast, but we find many examples of people fasting for spiritual reasons in the Bible. Matthew 4:1–2 says Jesus fasted for forty days and forty nights in the wilderness. This was a time of testing and preparation for three years in ministry. In many versions of Matthew and Mark, Jesus said some unclean spirits can only come out by fasting and prayer.[11] In the Old Testament, the Jews were commanded to fast on one day of the year: the Day of Atonement.[12] Fasting was about discipline, transformation, turning away from sin. Sometimes men, such as Daniel[13] and David,[14] fasted to strengthen their faith and spiritual awareness.

Esther fasted for a specific reason: to prepare to approach and convince King Xerxes to change his order to annihilate the Jews. Her three days of fasting was to clarify her focus and strengthen her mind, body, heart, and spirit for what was to come. For Esther, fasting was about preparing for a specific event that meant life or death for the entire Jewish race.

What to Do

Learn about the purpose and practice of fasting, and consider its role in your relationship with God. How might fasting prepare you for an upcoming event or season? Fasting isn't for everyone and can be harmful for certain people, so carefully consider your physical health. Also, fasting doesn't have to be a strict "no food, no water" time of testing. Sometimes people fast from specific types of food (e.g., animal products, coffee, sugar) or activities (e.g., complaining, surfing the internet, shopping).

If you fast, remember the purpose is to focus on God and experience internal change, not to convince Him to answer your prayers the way you want. Ideally, fasting strengthens you spiritually, fights dark forces, and aligns you with God's will for your life. When you fast, remember Jesus' experience in the wilderness. He was tested several times and He declared Scripture out loud. The Holy Spirit led Jesus into a new season of life.

Blossoming in Leadership

The home invasion—and the parable about tying up your camel and trusting God—taught me how to balance action and faith. I was good at preparing, planning, and taking action, but not so good at trusting God or planting my identity in Jesus.

Take, for example, my repeated refusal to lead when God called. He kept lobbing leadership roles my way, and I kept dodging them. Or I'd catch them, then drop them. At the University of Alberta, I was the president of the Undergraduate Psychology Association. When I taught in Africa, I was the team leader of the eighth-grade teachers. At home I created a variety of Bible studies, book clubs, writers' and artists' groups. Within a year I'd abandon them because I got scared of leading. *Who do I think I am, anyway? A queen? I'm nothing. I can't do this.*

Here's the problem: It was all about *me.* I was consumed by other people's reactions, opinions, and thoughts of me. My identity was defined by how many people showed up or dropped out, liked or disliked, opted in or out. The solution? I had to work through my fear and insecurity to receive love and self-worth from God. That's how I found freedom from my tired old attachments to outcomes and opinions. Now I happily create and lead, and my identity isn't affected by negative or positive responses.

"See, I am doing a new thing!" says the Lord. "Now it springs up; do you not perceive it? I am making a way in the wilderness and streams in the wasteland."[15] My life changed when I rooted my identity in God, freely shared what I was given, and moved forward in faith. And so did Esther's.

Esther Blossoms

In biblical times, queens—even beautiful, charming ones—wouldn't see their husbands for weeks or months. Esther was brought to King Xerxes' chamber for the occasional overnight visit. She made appearances for official events, dinners, celebrations. She wasn't permitted to visit the royal chambers unannounced or discuss political affairs, such as Haman's plan to exterminate the Jews. The annihilation was a formal edict signed and sealed by King Xerxes; it wasn't a topic for Esther to consider, much less challenge.

So, by suggesting she approach Xerxes, Mordecai was asking Esther to risk her life.

Not only did Esther rise to the occasion, she owned it! She started with, "But the king will put me to death if I approach his throne without permission." And then she blossomed into, "If I perish, I perish."[16] What caused this dramatic shift in character and courage? How did our Jewish orphan Hadassah become smart, strong Queen Esther?

She realized it was no longer about *her*. She now had a greater purpose, something to live and die for. She grew from obedient, compliant Hadassah to determined, strong, courageous Queen Esther. She stopped taking orders and started leading. Esther told Mordecai to fast for three days and to instruct all the Jews to do the same. She directed her attendants to fast and told the royal kitchen to prepare a series of banquets. Our biblical sister used her resources, rallied her troops, and strengthened her resolve. Esther became the woman God created her to be, refusing to limit herself to who she had been in the past.

You and I may not have royal positions, but we are growing into ourselves. The final Blossom Tip in this chapter shows us how to peel off the wrong labels and affix the right ones.

BRAIN BLOSSOM—
Labels

Sometimes we can't see our own potential or appreciate our abilities because we're scared of what people think. We're afraid of rejection and excommunication. This is natural; we're hard-wired to protect ourselves. For centuries, people would literally die if they were cast out of the tribe or clan. So our instincts and social conditioning—especially as women—make us want to fit in. We're like bottles of possibility, fizzy and frothy inside but insecure and scared we'll explode and make a mess.

What if we could look at ourselves from the outside and see what others see?

"What is written on every single one of your bottles are words and phrases and truths more powerful than you can imagine," writes James L. Rubart in the novel *The Long Journey to Jake Palmer*. "If you knew what was written there, right there on your label, if you truly knew what other people think of you, if you truly knew the impact you have on them, you would be stunned."[7]

What to Do

Imagine you're a bottle with a label you can't see. Is your bottle big and shapely, like a Fiasco jug of bold wine? Or maybe you're a ceramic bottle of fresh milk, or a cylindrical jar of spicy salsa. Picture your label—maybe it's colorful and eye-catching, or spare and understated. Maybe it's detailed and wordy, or simple and clear.

How can you see what's written on your label? Two suggestions: (1) Look back on your life and note the opportunities that keep appearing. (2) Share this exercise with someone you trust and ask for insight. What abilities, gifts, and aptitudes do they see in you? How are you preventing yourself from growing and flourishing? Invite the Holy Spirit into your reflections. Ask God to guide you into the next season and help you blossom into the woman He wants you to be.

QUESTIONS *for* JOURNALING *and* DISCUSSION

1. **What Then?** How do you deal with fear and anxiety? What stops you from relying on Jesus with 100 percent faith and trust?

2. **Your Secrets:** What secrets are you keeping out of fear or shame? What do you share openly? Describe how it might feel to tell a secret you've never told.

3. **God's Secrets:** Where and when are you most overwhelmed by God's creativity and imagination?

4. **Fast Times:** What is your experience with fasting? Did it change you or your relationship with God?

5. **Labels:** What do you have trouble believing or accepting about yourself? When have you walked away from opportunities you were afraid to pursue?

How are you? If you feel upset by anything in this chapter, reach out for in-person support. Talk to someone you trust or call a counselor. I don't give personal advice or counseling, but you may find it helpful to share your thoughts on my *She Blossoms* blog. As always, your comments are welcome at BlossomTips.com/Esther.

Growing Forward

Our next biblical sister, Mary Magdalene, blossomed into who God created her to be—but only after Jesus healed her. Let's see how He guided her through the dark, stormy nights into a new season of life and freedom.

9

Growing Forward with Mary Magdalene

Mary of Magdala didn't start out free or healthy. Even after Jesus healed her, she had to shift her self-image and receive a new life with an open heart and willing hands. The Blossom Tips planted in this chapter will help you do the same. Starting with tiny seeds, we'll end with a fresh way to look at our old goals.

Not So Witchy After All

It took me seven years to introduce my husband to my mom. I wasn't comfortable with her appearance; her hair is long and gray, and she's missing a few teeth (the dental bridge hurts her mouth). Her clothes are bedraggled, often held together by safety pins. She tends to stare at people for longer than necessary, breathing loudly and rhythmically at random points during conversations. She doesn't pluck her chin hairs and her back is starting to hunch over.

On the upside, my mom is thrilled about mundane events. It's contagious! She's overjoyed when I call every Sunday evening. She loves eating good food, listening to the radio, going to church. She was recently moved to a group home for elderly adults with mental health issues. She doesn't enjoy the constant presence of other people, but her social workers worried about her safety. The last time she lived alone she fell asleep with a lit cigarette in her mouth and started her apartment on fire. My mom almost never complains, knowing she's safe and cared for. She always ends our conversations the same exuberant way: "Will you call me next week? I love you, Laurie!"

Bruce liked my mom when he finally met her. His perspective helped me accept her—and myself—with more compassion, kindness, and love. Even so, if they meet again I'll still feel little-girl scared. My mom's schizophrenia is under control, but uncured. She's unpredictable, after sixty years of powerful antipsychotic medications and shock treatments. My mom probably won't blossom into the woman God created her to be until she meets Him face-to-face in heaven.

I can't wait to see her there.

How They Saw Her

Mary Magdalene became who God created her to be—but only after Jesus cast "seven demons" out of her.[1] Some scholars believe she wasn't literally possessed by evil spirits or the devil; she may have been suffering from a seizure disorder such as schizophrenia or epilepsy.[2] However, Mary's specific illness didn't matter to Jesus; His love and acceptance knew no boundaries.

I often wonder how Mary's illness affected the townspeople in her fishing village of Magdala. Maybe they avoided or ostracized her because of her affliction or resulting behavior. Sick people are treated differently, especially if they struggle with a mental health issue like schizophrenia. Perhaps people pitied Mary, or felt uncomfortable or frightened if she behaved unpredictably. Maybe they saw her as unclean.

Some scholars believe Mary Magdalene was an older, wealthy widow who was Jesus' companion and confidante.[3] They agree she was a faithful disciple who helped support Jesus' ministry with her own financial resources.

After Jesus cured Mary, her self-perception must have changed. She had to let go of her old habits of thinking and being so she could become a new woman. This might not have been easy for our biblical sister, especially if it was an instantaneous healing. Her mind and emotions needed time to catch up. Similarly, the people who knew the "old Mary" had to adjust their perspective of her. She had to grow into her new self, trusting who Jesus said she was and allowing her life to move forward in a new direction.

Jesus planted new seeds in Mary Magdalene's life, but she needed to nurture them. He does the same for us today, sowing seeds like the Blossom Tips below, helping us to sprout and flourish.

SPIRIT BLOSSOM—
Seeds

When bad seeds are planted, they die—or they multiply like life-choking weeds. Those weeds can tarnish a reputation for centuries, much like the old myths about Mary Magdalene. Unsavory rumors can begin with lies or even slight exaggerations of the truth. Those rumors, if they take hold, grow and eventually become destructive forces of shame and guilt.

What rumors or myths have you heard about yourself or others? Maybe you unknowingly influence what people think and say about you. Perhaps you say things like, "I'm not spiritual or good enough to pray out loud in a group," or "I don't deserve a job promotion or raise." Perhaps you stand aside while rumors are spread about others, or you unthinkingly contribute to other people's reputations by saying things like, "Eve is always late, which disrupts every meeting! Bless her soul."

It's time to nurture new seeds.

What to Do

Think about who you were a year ago, or even last month. What did you believe about yourself? Was it true? How have you changed, and how is Jesus growing you? For example, my feelings of unworthiness grew from childhood seeds that germinated and became weeds. Then Jesus sowed seeds of truth, grace, and freedom. My task is to cultivate the life-giving sprouts and weed out the thorns.

What fresh, holy seeds are being planted in your life? Ask God to show you the next step. You don't need to see the whole garden or season. Nurture and grow your seeds, and they'll flourish. Notice the fresh green sprouts, and give them your time and energy! Hold them up to Jesus and receive His light, power, and strength. Share your ideas, hopes, and dreams with Christians who can help you grow. Work with God—the Gardener—as He blossoms you.

My Underlying Motivation

The real reason I didn't want Bruce to meet my mom was my image. I wanted to control what he (and everyone) thought of me. The thought of my mom meeting Bruce, his huge Catholic family, and my friends at our wedding—the "happiest day of my life"—was inconceivable. So I didn't invite my parents. My sister declined my invitation, and I had no other relatives. Our wedding took place in Bruce's family's church, officiated by a priest I'd never met. I'm not Catholic, but I wanted to please my mother-in-law. The icing on the cake? I dislike being in the spotlight and never cared about a big wedding. I joked about eloping and being married by a fake Elvis in Las Vegas, but I wasn't kidding.

I was forgetting something important: Bruce and I are kindred spirits. Our relationship, which started as a friendship seventeen years before we married, is built on a foundation of love, trust, and support. I didn't know our marriage could weather the storms of unpredictable schizophrenic mothers, family expectations, and Catholic formalities until we experienced those seasons together.

In general, kindred spirits are more than friends but not always lovers. Kindred spirits "get" each other. Regardless of their age, gender, background, job, or income level, kindred spirits have a connection that sprouts quickly and grows forever. They support each other through life's highs and lows. Kindred spirits can spend hours climbing Mount Everest, waiting for chemotherapy cocktails to drip through IV tubes, or quietly reading in front of the fireplace.

I believe Jesus and Mary Magdalene were kindred spirits.

Mary Magdalene and Jesus

"Mary," said Jesus—and she knew it was Him. She couldn't see clearly through her puffy eyes, red and swollen from days of crying. She didn't recognize His physical appearance; there was something different about Him, perhaps because He'd been dead for days and was resurrected in a new form. Mary believed Jesus' body still lay dead; she never dreamed He was alive.

Yet when He said her name, she knew.

Mary Magdalene was there for Jesus in ways nobody else was. She stayed by His side through the whole bloody ordeal. She remained at the foot of the cross and witnessed His torture, crucifixion, and death. She went to the tomb to anoint His body with spices, and kept returning even after His body disappeared. Mary was loyal and faithful to Jesus despite her grief, confusion, and disappointment. She was present, active, and available. And Jesus met her right where she was.

Kindred spirits show up for each other even when "there" is the most painful place on earth. They're willing to keep hoping, trusting, and believing even when people are cruel and life hurts. Kindred spirits love each other in practical ways, whether they're grieving or celebrating.

Happily, kindred spirits aren't as rare as you might think. It doesn't always take years to bond with a new friend. Remember how Jesus' disciples responded to His invitation? They immediately dropped everything to follow Him. They *knew*. Our next Blossom Tip shows us how we, too, can recognize and develop close relationships.

HEART BLOSSOM—
Kindred Spirits

The dictionary says kindred spirits have "similar interests, beliefs, attitudes, and hobbies." Yes, but let's dig deeper. Kindred spirits offer comforting "you get me" feelings of being known, understood, accepted. You may not agree on everything, but you feel understood and accepted. That person—or pet dog, cat, horse, bird—is part of your soul. You never lose that connection, even when they're no longer around physically. Kindred spirits start their relationships on earth and perfect them in heaven.

Jesus is your kindred spirit. He knows your name just as intimately as He did Mary's. He accepts your feelings, problems, and fears. He knows what you need, and what you *think* you need. He knows what you'll face today, tomorrow, and next year. Maybe you don't recognize Jesus right now because your eyes are blinded by tears of grief or loneliness, but He's here.

What to Do

Remember that kindred spirits come in surprising shapes, sizes, and forms! I've found kindred spirits in the Bible, in book characters, in dogs, and in fellow travelers in Jerusalem. Don't discount a possible kindred spirit because she's older, younger, prettier, more talented, or wealthier. Look beneath her appearance and see if there's a friendship waiting to be discovered.

Nurture new friendships like you'd tend freshly planted seeds or tiny green sprouts. Include Jesus in your conversations and activities, sprinkling His truth and light in your interactions. When your season comes to a conclusion (and all seasons must end), let them go with grace and love. Know that you will see into them again one day—if not here on earth, then in heaven.

Holding It All Loosely

One drawback of moving in and out of foster homes is the loss of stuff. I didn't have much to begin with: I remember a white bunny with floppy satin ears, a small pink purse containing fifty cents, a few tangle-haired blond Barbie dolls. When the social worker came to move me in or out, I'd throw my belongings in a black plastic garbage bag. My mom never took me back to the place we lived before the foster home. She just left the apartment behind with everything in it. Today, my only childhood possessions are a few photos and small diaries.

On the bright side, I have no attachment to stuff! This doesn't thrill my husband; he's a "save it for a rainy day" kind of guy. We're definitely not kindred spirits on the "stuff" issue. "You never know when it might come in handy," Bruce says, carefully packing away the TV set he bought at a thrift store in 1984. "Someday we'll be glad we have it."

I don't usually enjoy receiving birthday or Christmas gifts, especially if they're material possessions. Kitchen and garden gadgets aren't my thing either—I'll cheerfully use a soup spoon to dig up potatoes in the garden (making gift-giving a dilemma for Bruce, not to mention finding clean soup spoons at lunch!). I do, however, struggle with money. I always thought if I had enough money I'd feel secure. The more I have in the bank, the safer I think I am. This is a valley that Jesus is walking me through.

Mary Magdalene didn't seem to have my financial struggles. Indeed, she and Jesus were kindred spirits when it came to money.

Mary Magdalene's Stuff

Meeting Jesus changed Mary's life in every way—including how she handled her money and possessions. Mary had stuff, but she wasn't attached to it. Bible commentators say she was a wealthy woman; her village was a popular source of Israel's sought-after salted fish that was exported around the Mediterranean. "Thus Magdala was probably an affluent town," writes T. J. Wray in *Good Girls, Bad Girls of the New Testament*, "and Mary, assigned the town's very name in biblical references to her, likely comes from a family of means."[4]

Mary Magdalene left her family, friends, and home in that thriving, safe fishing village. What did people think about her traveling from place to place with Jesus and His disciples, listening to Him teach, supporting His work, and offering her financial and material resources? She came from a world of comfort, power, and social status . . . and yet she didn't hoard her money or possessions. She didn't choose a safe, easy, low-risk way of life. Luke 8 says Jesus' female followers not only followed Him, they helped finance His ministry. Mary wasn't trailing after Jesus like a fan or groupie; she used her possessions, money, and other resources to serve Him in practical ways.

Mary Magdalene didn't just profess her faith; she *lived in faith* by pouring her wealth and reputation into a ministry she knew was true. She held her possessions, lifestyle, and society's expectations with open hands—which is exactly how we, too, can live and blossom.

SOUL BLOSSOM—
Open Hands

Every three months I get a call from Big Brothers/Big Sisters. They're a nonprofit mentoring organization that matches youth from low-income, single-parent households with adult volunteers. In fact, I was a Little Sister when I was eleven years old—and I'm still friends with my Big Sister today, thirty-five years later! I've been volunteering as a Big Sister for seven years. My Little Sister is now eighteen years old.

The Big Brothers organization in my city accepts donations of clothing, books, video games, and various household items. They sell those donations to Value Village, raising money to run the organization and monitor Big/Little relationships. I love this easy, effective way to reduce clutter: Big Brothers calls when the truck is coming to my neighborhood, and I leave my donation in front of the house.

What to Do

Sort through your stuff on a regular basis. Don't keep saying you'll "get to it someday," because that day never comes. Find a local nonprofit organization that has a partnership with a thrift store. Ideally, they'll call you regularly when a donation truck is coming to your area. A regular pickup schedule will motivate you to sort through your closets, drawers, garage, and basement for possessions you no longer need or want.

Set up a couple of boxes, bins, or bags somewhere visible in your home. Those are your "Open Hands" boxes. Take fifteen or thirty minutes every week to go through your stuff and create fresh, clean space. Check the organization's list of acceptable items; don't donate broken, ripped, or stained items. Decluttering your piles will help you sort through the past and eliminate what you no longer need. It'll also give you physical, emotional, and spiritual room to breathe.

Riding Free at Last

Shortly after I turned seventeen I moved into my own apartment. No more foster homes, social workers, crazy mother—I was free at last! I waitressed at a pancake house while finishing high school. My wild adventures included grocery shopping, cooking my favorite foods, and riding my bike to the library.

I loved my independence so much that I turned away from Jesus. I knew He had plans for me, but I didn't want *anyone* telling me what to do. Not even God. I prayed every night, but silently and really really fast. It didn't count.

Then Jesus swept through my life, knocking me to my knees with a poem called "The Road of Life" by Tim Hansel. I loved the image of riding a tandem bike with Jesus in the front seat! He takes us on adventures I could never imagine. We pause at pinnacles to marvel at our Father's snow-covered mountaintops, lush green valleys, winding blue rivers. I cling to Jesus as we fly down stomach-dropping, bluff-hugging roads and navigate hairpin turns, descending into deep canyons. Scary. Thrilling! Jesus doesn't say where we're going. I fear not.

Yes, I struggle through dark valleys and dry deserts. Yes, I have to sweat and pedal. No, Jesus doesn't do all the work. But He always gets on first and motions me over. Once I'm on, He leans back a little. I lean forward. Jesus whispers, "I have something to show you!" He winks and *zoom*, off we go on a new adventure.

Mary Magdalene's Adventures

Jesus didn't force Mary or any of His followers to go on His road trips. He *invited* them. "Come, follow me!" And away they went, without the luxury of bikes, GPS maps, weather forecasts, or hotels. They didn't even have the reassuring presence of the Holy Spirit.

Mary Magdalene was free to leave Jesus any time. She could have walked away when He was dying on the cross, or after He was

171

laid in the tomb. She could have walked away when her heart was shattered by grief, disbelief, confusion—not to mention the horror and trauma of watching her beloved friend die. She could have walked away when the disciples doubted her testimony or when she saw angels sitting in Jesus' tomb. But she didn't. Her love and devotion overpowered everything, even her fear and pain.

When Jesus spoke her name, Mary knew it was Him. He was inviting her on yet another adventure, one that required courage, faith, and resolve. Mary Magdalene was about to embark on the most difficult and unbelievable season of her life. She never could have planned or prepared for it . . . but she didn't have to. Jesus was guiding her every step of the way, always pouring His strength and presence into her life.

Even with Jesus powering us through the cold valleys and hot deserts, the journey can feel endless and exhausting. Our energy fades, spirits dim, emotions overwhelm. But Jesus doesn't just help us pedal. He packs provisions to sustain our bodies—like manna from heaven—and helps us grow along the way.

BODY BLOSSOM—
Manna

Once a week I dive into a giant yellow bowl of salty buttered popcorn for dinner. That's it. Just a tub of popcorn, all for me. Food is freedom to me—and I treasure the gift of buying whatever I want at the grocery store. Growing up, I ate too many ketchup-and-mustard sandwiches and cold hot dogs. It wasn't until I was in my twenties that I realized I don't even *like* hot dogs. Or ketchup-and-mustard sandwiches.

I marvel at God's gift of food. We're blessed with an endless array of tastes, aromas, textures, and types of food. Crispy yam fries hot out of the oven, thick pumpkin and cinnamon soup, rich tomato sauce on angel hair pasta, fresh sweet chunks of pineapple and mango. *And that's just one meal.* We get to eat three times a day—plus snacks! Food is everything at once: delicious, energizing, healing, and life-giving. Manna from heaven.

What to Do

Taste the freedom. Fix a delicious meal—a single dish, a dessert, a five-course dinner—that delights you. Maybe you relish roast turkey with mashed potatoes and gravy; a hot, wood-fired pizza with sharp feta cheese, tomatoes, and spinach; or fresh rainbow trout grilled over an open fire. Make it, bake it, take it! Enjoy it with friends or savor it quietly. Taste the flavors. Pause to take pleasure. Pretend you're having a picnic with Jesus after a long bike ride.

Reconsider your relationship with food; consider making it a symbol of a fresh new beginning in your life. Experiment with different recipes, unusual flavor pairings, interesting new cookbooks. Above all, remember God when you ponder the endless variety, abundance, textures, colors, flavors, and smells. Taste and take joy! Raise your glass to Jesus.

Growing into a New Season

It took me a long time—almost twenty years—to tell people that I lived in foster homes as a child. I thought I was the only kid in the world with a schizophrenic mom. I built thick walls around my heart, burying my secrets and allowing shame and unworthiness to control my self-identity. Telling people, even my husband and closest friends, felt impossible because it was all about *me*. I cared so much what people thought that I couldn't be honest about who I was. I was protecting my image, pride, and identity.

Also, I wanted to avoid people's pity and judgment. Mental illness isn't highly regarded or understood, even by people who personally experienced schizophrenia, depression, anxiety disorders, or other health struggles. Schizophrenia is an intense, frightening disorder that leads to unpredictable and sometimes harmful behavior. I didn't want to be associated with it in any way. I also didn't want people to think I, too, was schizophrenic.

Even when I began to understand myself intellectually, my heart didn't change overnight. I couldn't stop pushing people away, protecting myself, hiding behind walls. I didn't want to lose control by revealing who I really was. I also didn't know *how* to be authentic; all I knew was to shield my heart and bury my spirit.

God softened my heart, slowly massaging His love and healing into my soul. He spoke through the podcast sermons I listened to on my daily walks. He planted the seeds, and I nurtured my relationship with Jesus through the Holy Spirit. Eventually, I realized I'm part of God's big picture. It's not my story . . . it's His.

Mary Plants Fresh Seeds

"Do not hold on to me, for I have not yet ascended to the Father," Jesus said to Mary, "go instead to my brothers and tell them, 'I am ascending to my Father and your Father, and to my God and your God.'"[5]

Jesus didn't accidentally happen to bump into Mary Magdalene before seeing His other followers and disciples. God *chose* her—a woman!—to be the first person to see Jesus after the resurrection. In Jewish culture back then, women weren't allowed to speak in courts of law and were seen as unreliable witnesses. A woman's testimony wasn't trustworthy because of her low social status.

And yet Jesus trusted Mary Magdalene to be the first human to share His message with the world. This was His plan for her, and for the world. I wonder if she remembered Isaiah 43:19: "See, I am doing a new thing! Now it springs up; do you not perceive it? I am making a way in the wilderness and streams in the wasteland."

Jesus didn't choose Mary because she was perfect. He chose her because of her faith and willingness to move forward into a new life. Mary went to the disciples and became the first woman to declare the risen Jesus, simply by sharing what she saw and heard.

Not only did Jesus give Mary an assignment, He said it wasn't time to hold on to Him. Now she had a new focus and different goals: to hear His word and pass it along. Jesus and Mary Magdalene's time together on earth was over. There was no going back. She didn't get to choose when her season with Jesus on earth began or ended, but she could choose how to move forward into the next chapter of her life.

When God ushers you into a new season, you get to decide how you'll move through it. Your old goals probably need to be revisited, revised, perhaps even rejected. In this chapter's last Blossom Tip, you'll learn how to "regoal" when your original plans have evaporated.

BRAIN BLOSSOM—
Regoaling

Sometimes a new direction in life is unexpected and shocking; other times, it's anticipated and even planned. Either way, change requires an adjustment of plans and expectations. Regoaling is a deliberate choice to release an old goal and move in a new direction. It's a conscious decision to refocus your energy and change your course. Regoaling requires you to accept that your original goal is unachievable, unrealistic, or undesirable, and to commit wholeheartedly to a new purpose and plan.

When she met Jesus, Mary's goal was to travel with Him and support His ministry. This goal became impossible after His crucifixion. Her goal then became to anoint His body with spices and prepare Him for burial. That goal also unexpectedly and quickly changed! Jesus gave her a fresh new focus for her life: to spread His gospel by sharing what she saw, heard, and experienced. Mary regrouped and regoaled.

What to Do

Consider a goal you once had that is now unattainable. Maybe your plan was to live in a certain place with a specific person for the rest of your life. Or perhaps you expected to be married with children and have family vacations, holiday dinners, and birthday celebrations. Maybe you experienced a loss or disappointment that brought your life to a screeching halt. You're struggling to survive this season because your heart keeps looking back.

Decide that the time has come for you to regoal. Choose to be an active participant, not a reluctant bystander. How will you walk forward into the next season? Maybe you need professional advice from a lawyer, doctor, accountant, or career coach. Perhaps you need to learn how to set measurable, realistic, timely, actionable goals. Go slow, be specific, and stay focused. Enter a new season with curiosity, armed with God's Spirit, love, and strength. You're part of His story, and you're growing forward.

1. **Seeds:** What good and bad seeds were planted in your life or heart long ago? How did they affect your perspective, choices, and self-identity?

2. **Kindred Spirits:** Whom have you loved, and lost? Describe two or three people you're currently close to. What makes them kindred spirits?

3. **Open Hands:** Where are you on a Stuff Scale of 1 to 10 (1 = Minimalist and 10 = Hoarder)? How do you feel about decluttering your closets, drawers, garage, or basement?

4. **Manna:** How would you describe your relationship with food, cooking, and eating? How often do you eat mindlessly, using food to soothe your fears or anxieties?

5. **Regoaling:** What three steps could you take toward a new goal in your life? What financial, emotional, social, or spiritual resources do you need?

How is your journey unfolding? Come, share your experience with me at BlossomTips.com/MaryMagdalene.

Growing Forward

Our season together is ending, and we're entering our final chapter. Who better than Mary of Nazareth to take us home?

Jesus' own mother, the woman who birthed and raised Him. She encouraged and supported Him through His journey. She was there when He said, "It is finished."[6] Mary shows us what it *really* means to blossom in God's love, power, and faith.

10

Blossoming into Life with Mary

All together now! In our final chapter, we blend the strength and wisdom of the ages by gathering all our biblical sisters. We embrace Mary of Nazareth and honor her past. We also cherish the present while continuing to walk humbly and confidently into the future God has planned for us.

All the Ways to Say Yes

In the beginning, Eve said yes by accepting her losses and choosing to praise God for fresh blessings in new seasons. Sarah said an unorthodox yes by marching ahead of the Lord and attempting to fulfill His promises her way. Undaunted, God wove her version of "surrender" into His story; Sarah and Abraham's children remained part of His plan.

Hagar said yes—after fleeing, fearing, and fretting. She accepted God's provisions and let Him lead her and Ishmael home. Naomi and Ruth said yes by moving through fear, doubt, and uncertainty while starting over as widows in Israel. Ruth repeatedly said yes by pledging her allegiance to God, turning away from Moabite idols, gleaning, and risking her life by approaching Boaz. She became King David's great-grandmother.

Martha said yes by welcoming and feeding people in her home. Her sister, Mary, said yes by sitting and learning at Jesus' feet. Hannah said yes by expressing her grief and setting her heart on God's will for her life. God gave her Samuel, whom she gave back to Him.

Queen Esther said yes by fasting, dressing in her most fetching garments, and preparing delicious feasts. She captivated and convinced King Xerxes to spare the lives of the Jews. Mary Magdalene said yes, yes, and *yes!* to Jesus' healing, friendship, and call on her life.

Our biblical sisters surrendered to God in different ways, depending on their position, personality, and predicament. No two lives were the same, except for one thing: They all said yes.

How Mary Said Yes

Mary of Nazareth was the Jewish mother of Jesus. She is lauded as the Blessed Virgin Mary, Saint Mary, Madonna. She was faithful, courageous, and strong—but she was also a real woman who faced great pain, sacrifice, and grief. She loved her husband, Joseph, and her son, Jesus. She lost them both.

When we meet Mary in the first chapter of Luke, she is about fourteen years old. She was puzzled and disturbed when the angel Gabriel appeared and said she was favored by God. Her baby Jesus would be great, the Son of the Most High, reigning over a never-ending kingdom.[1] Mary contemplated Gabriel's words and calmly asked how the Messiah could be born of her, a virgin. She was baffled and curious but didn't allow doubt or fear to overwhelm her.

Mary actively chose to participate in God's plans. Soon after her conversation with Gabriel, she hurried to Elizabeth's home in Judea. This wasn't an overnight trip; it involved days of walking or riding a donkey, perhaps alone. Was her relative Elizabeth also pregnant, as Gabriel said? Yes! Unborn John the Baptist leapt in Elizabeth's womb at the sound of Mary's voice. She sang the Magnificat in praise and gratitude.

Mary, like Hannah centuries earlier, sang *yes!* to God even though she had no idea what her future held. She said yes to the possibility of losing her fiancé and living in disgrace as an unwed mother. She said yes to an unknown, unchosen new season in her life. Mary had no idea what she was agreeing to, and yet she blossomed into the biggest yes of her life.

SPIRIT BLOSSOM—

Saying Yes

Saying yes is easier said than done, unless we're accepting a second helping of chocolate brownie delight. "Thank you, Jesus, don't mind if I do!" Making room for another scoop of goodness doesn't take much faith or courage. Not as easy, however, is accepting another loss, obstacle, disappointment, or test. We know we should say yes to God. We may even *want* to say yes because deep down we know His plans are good. But what if saying yes is painful, confusing, or difficult?

We must allow our relationship with God to change. For example, what we understood about God last year (or last night) is different today because X happened. X might be the thing we fear we will never get over. X knocked us over or broke our heart.

But even though X hurts, it has the potential to re-create and strengthen our relationship with God.

What to Do

Rebuild your faith. Your journey with God started with simple, untested beliefs. Now that you've experienced real life (X) with Him, you can grow into a deeper, richer relationship. Accept that your faith is being tested by the natural, inevitable storms of life, time, and people. Not to mention Satan's use of anything from chocolate to terror attacks to weaken your relationship with Jesus.

Recall a painful X in your life. Maybe you don't have to cast far back in your memory; maybe you're going through X right now. Is your faith growing deeper and closer to Jesus, or dimmer and farther away? If you feel far from God, know that reconnection is moments away. Remember that all relationships involve periods of distance and closeness, silence and recommitment. It's okay; you can rebuild. Reconnecting with Jesus can be as simple as taking a deep breath and turning your heart and mind to Him.

God Only Knows

Sometimes we have to wrestle with "Why?" before we get to yes. I struggled with "Why me?" when I was young, trying to make sense of my mad mother. My childhood was a roller coaster of breakneck speeds and drops of doom, with few thrilling heights.

"You were a mistake, and I almost put you up for adoption," my mom said. "I lived in a home for unwed mothers. They told me to give you away because it'd be impossible to raise you alone."

I often wished my mom *had* given me away. I yearned for normal parents, pets, ice-skating lessons. My foster homes were almost too good; living with families made it hard to move back with my mother. And I felt bad for my foster siblings, whose lives were hard. Baby Clayton was born addicted to heroin because his mom was an addict. Wild teen Dakota kept running away with her boyfriend, who kept beating her up. "Why, God?" I asked on everyone's behalf.

As an adult, living in Kenya also perplexed me. Why was I born a white girl in Canada while my black house worker was born under a dirty tarp in a Kenyan field? My African friends would have given their right arm to have had my "difficult childhood." They couldn't go to school, search for a purpose-driven life, or take time to grieve loss. They needed clean water, food, medicine, safety.

I'm not the only one who asked God why. On the cross Jesus asked, "Why have you forsaken me?"[2]

Mary Let God Be God

Mary didn't ask Gabriel why the Lord chose her. We don't know if she ever questioned God—though she did ask twelve-year-old Jesus why He stayed in Jerusalem without telling her and Joseph. In turn, Jesus asked Mary why she was worried. Where else would He be, but His Father's house?[3]

Since Joseph wasn't mentioned after that incident, he likely wasn't around during Jesus' ministry. Mary was probably widowed, which explains why Jesus on the cross asked John to take care of her.[4] She didn't have a husband. "Why, God?" I asked on Mary's behalf. "She lost her son, she was faithful to you, she said yes. Why couldn't she at least grow old with Joseph as her life partner?"

Maybe God chose Mary of Nazareth because she didn't ask such questions. She was courageous, open-minded, and willing to trust Him. She didn't let fear or doubt distract her from living wholeheartedly. She didn't hesitate to ask for help, such as by calling Jesus when wine was running low at a wedding celebration.[5] When He didn't immediately acquiesce, she didn't complain, argue, or resist. Mary's attitude was always, "Your will be done."

Perhaps God chose Mary because she was willing to accept Him for who He was. She didn't try to control Jesus or insist that life unfold her way. Mary let God be God, which freed her to be herself. Not a perfect woman or sinless mother. Just Mary, a woman from Nazareth.

When we accept God for who He is, we free ourselves to flourish into who we are.

HEART BLOSSOM—

Becoming You

You aren't called to be Mary (or Hannah, or Esther). Jesus calls you to become who He created *you* to be. He reveals the lives of our biblical sisters to help us learn and grow. We see their strengths and weaknesses, successes and failures. We witness God's work in their lives and see how His plans unfolded to fulfill His purpose.

While we don't want to be them, our biblical sisters had qualities we ought to nurture. Mary of Nazareth was receptive and courageous; Mary of Bethany was sensitive and teachable. Martha was hospitable and expressive, Ruth loyal and determined. Esther was a leader, Hagar a servant. Eve and Mary Magdalene had unique relationships with God. Each woman's life was part of His plan . . . and so are ours.

When you get to heaven, God won't ask, "Why weren't you more like Mary of Nazareth?" Instead He might ask, "Why weren't you more *you*?"

What to Do

Choose one or two biblical women who intrigue you. Who stands out? Look up specific verses related to her, and ask the Holy Spirit to reveal more. For example, Luke 2:19 says, "But Mary treasured up all these things and pondered them in her heart." You might ask these questions of this—or any—verse: What happened before and after? What does it say about God? About Mary? What did it mean back then? What is its timeless truth? How does this verse apply today? What is God saying to *you*? Think, write, and talk through your thoughts.

Ask God questions about your life. What are you struggling to accept or release? Do you need more focus, faith, or fearlessness? Don't ask Jesus to change your circumstances until you praise and worship Him for who He is. Ask Him to change your *heart*. God will respond to your prayers when you seek and trust Him.

Not Blossoming in All Seasons

I didn't blossom in Nairobi, Kenya. In fact, that three-year stint was the longest, most painful season of my life. I struggled to live with joy and peace among millions of poor, starving, oppressed people who dreamed of eating a daily meal of goat stew and chapati. I was anxious and insecure teaching eighth grade, even though the students were well-behaved and my teaching load was light. I struggled with being single at thirty-two with no eligible men to date. I attended weekly counseling sessions with a psychologist, and was emotionally drained from working through my past.

Instead of saying yes to God and adapting to a new season in life—like Esther in King Xerxes' palace—I succumbed to insecurity, doubt, and fear. I identified more with Naomi and isolated myself in loneliness and despair. Instead of leaning on God's strength and provisions like Hagar in the desert, I stayed blind with tears and grief. Instead of crying out like Hannah, who loved God for who He is despite her circumstances, I tried to succeed on my own. I, like Sarah, marched blindly and willfully ahead of God.

I just wanted to go home. I could have broken my teaching contract and moved back to Canada early, but I knew Africa was a season I had to experience. So I stayed the whole three years. I said, "Yes, your will be done," to God . . . and it was the hardest thing I've ever done.

Mary as a Woman

Mary was a daughter, wife, mother, and likely a widow. As a mom, she raised Jesus through many seasons of life. She was present at His birth and death. She, Jesus, and their family celebrated birthdays, weddings, Jewish holidays. She taught Jesus how to eat, do chores, socialize. They traveled to Jerusalem and perhaps Judea to visit Elizabeth and John. Jesus learned Judaic traditions and customs, studied Hebrew law, religion, psalms. He followed in His earthly father's footsteps by learning a trade. I love that Jesus had a happy, healthy childhood! "Jesus grew

186

in wisdom and stature, and in favor with God and man."[6] Mary was a good mom.

Then the season changed. Jesus started traveling and teaching, healing the faithful, and challenging the pious. His ministry carried Him away. One time Mary and her sons stood at the fringes of a crowd, unable to reach Jesus through all the people. Instead of going to them, Jesus said, "My mother and brothers are those who hear God's word and put it into practice."[7]

Mary was entering the season of her son as Savior. She watched Jesus grow into His role as Messiah, like she watched Him grow from newborn to toddler to teenager. This wasn't just an unfamiliar season for them as a family; it was uncharted territory for everyone.

When an unexpected, unpredictable season of life starts, we don't know how long it will last—or even how we'll survive. However, we do know two things: Jesus is weathering the storm with us, and even seasons of death contain seeds of life.

SOUL BLOSSOM—
T-Shirts and Totes

At home, the remaking of our bed is a sign of spring. We switch from winter's thick, warm sheets to springtime's lighter, flowery bedding. To me, this is a symbol of a fresh start. Even if I'm unprepared for spring, changing our bedding helps me adjust to the idea of a new season. A specific object or activity—as mundane as changing the sheets—can symbolize acceptance, surrender, and preparation for the future.

After Mary realized she and Elizabeth were both unexpectedly pregnant, she sang the Magnificat, a prayer marking the beginning of a new season in her life. Centuries earlier, Hannah sang a similar song to symbolize her transition from the old to the new. Our other biblical sisters honored new chapters in their lives in different ways. Esther, for example, fasted before embarking on a new season, and Naomi changed her name.

What to Do

Create a visual reminder that something significant has changed in your life. Maybe you're releasing a hope or accepting a loss. Maybe you're facing a new beginning with a mixture of fear and excitement. Perhaps you are grieving an ending and are struggling to move on. For better or worse, a fresh season has begun! Mark it by performing an activity or creating an object to help your mind, body, and heart adjust.

Make something to symbolize a new chapter in your life. For example, you might get colorful fabric paints and a plain white T-shirt or black tote bag. Paint something on your T-shirt or tote—it doesn't have to be anything specific. It could be your name in script, rainbow whooshes, or abstract spirals. It's not meant to be perfect or beautiful. It's simply your acknowledgment that a new season in your life has begun.

Surprised in the Valley

So many surprises awaited me in Africa, not all pleasant! Nairobi was a dangerous city with few cultural or social activities for ex-pats, especially single women. The sun set by 6:30 p.m. year-round. The poorly lit or completely dark streets, car-sized potholes, roaming bandits, and carjackers made driving dangerous. My fellow teachers, who also lived on the school's protected compound, were friendly, but I didn't enjoy evenings of watching movies or playing games. I felt alone, hiding behind walls of self-judgment and isolation. I read, wrote, and worked on my first artistic endeavor since kindergarten: a scrapbook.

And yet I look back on Africa as the richest, deepest experience of my life. I discovered I could survive a painful, seemingly endless season. I learned how to live one step at a time and show up when I wanted to run away and hide.

Delighting in the fruits of the season helped. I savored truckloads of Ngowe mangoes, Kenyan pineapples, fresh papaw. During school breaks I traveled to Ethiopia, Tanzania, Swaziland, and South Africa. I camped and biked in the Rift Valley, coasting slowly by herds of zebras and giraffe grazing on the roadside, pedaling madly past baboons and street hawkers. Evenings I'd gaze up at the inky black sky, lost in the unfamiliar patterns of planets, stars, and constellations.

God didn't randomly fling those stars across the night sky, and He didn't carelessly drop and abandon me in Africa. Now, looking back, I see He had a purpose for all the seasons in my life.

Mary's Valley of Shadows

Mary of Nazareth faced a season of death and grief no woman on earth has ever experienced—or ever will again. She had no idea what she was saying yes to when the angel Gabriel visited her. Mary knew she'd experience surprises as the Messiah's mom . . . but how could she ever prepare to witness her son Jesus' crucifixion and death on the cross?

"Mary's presence at such a frightening and traumatic event is difficult to imagine," writes T. J. Wray in *Good Girls, Bad Girls of the New Testament*. "Her beautiful son is beaten, bruised, and bleeding. She stands by, helpless in the face of Jesus' suffering, and must watch as he slowly dies before her eyes."[8]

Though she walked through the valley of the shadow of death, Mary remained steadfast and courageous. She was as willing at the foot of the cross as the day she met Gabriel thirty-three years earlier. Her love and faith were tested by time and trials, refined by God's presence and love. With Jesus she experienced weddings and funerals, healing and disease, joy and grief, blessings and loss. With God she lived, loved, and lost.

Mary's wholehearted faith carried her through the grief of her son's death, into a new season of life and ministry. In Acts 1:14, the Bible tells us she joined Peter and the apostles in prayer after Jesus died. Even after her son's death on the cross, Mary was still saying yes to God.

Saying yes to God means accepting all of life's surprises—good and bad, happy and sad. Some surprises spring from the world and even our own loved ones. Others rise unexpectedly from our own bodies, as we see in our penultimate Blossom Tip.

BODY BLOSSOM—
Surprise!

Saying yes to God always brings surprises, both delightful and distressing. We'll feel awed and humbled by His presence, joyfully discovering His love layered thick through the adventures. We'll be flabbergasted and hurt by family, friends, colleagues, pets, and life in general. Our bodies and minds will bewilder and even shock us. We must anticipate times of pain and healing, disease and health, death and life.

Expect the unexpected! Yesterday my dog Georgie heard a short, sharp noise behind her. Startled, she jerked around to see

190

what was creeping up. Nothing was there. She then lifted her snout in the air, nostrils twitching madly. *What is that* smell? I could see her thinking. *Ewww, gross. Let's get out of here!* Georgie had farted and was completely surprised by her own body. Then off she scampered, forgetting the past and trotting into the future.

What to Do

Use your body as a way to physically say yes to God. Dance and twirl in prayer and worship, or kneel with your forehead on the ground. Walk mindfully through a park or forest, seeing His handiwork in the flowers and rocks, birds and branches. Look up and blow God a kiss! Laugh and wink at Him when something silly happens, like your dog tooting. Remember how Jesus lounged as He ate and drank, how He walked on water, how He washed His disciples' feet. God can be physical, not just spiritual. Everything around us points to Him, including the delightful and dreadful shocks of our bodies and lives.

Expect your body to surprise you. Treat your whole body with respect, as a gift from God—even the stinky surprises and weird discharges. Take loving care of your aching and broken bits. Use the Sabbath to rest and renew your whole self as part of God's holy, beautiful creation.

In Season

If I had to relive my three-year stint in Africa, I'd do three things differently.

First, I'd amend my belief that everything is about *me*—moody students and distracted parents, cat-sized rats and bats, the revolving door of missionaries and visitors who took pieces of my heart home with them. I'd accept disappointments and pain as a natural part of life, without sinking into despair or self-loathing. I'd savor unexpected discoveries such as gecko eggs (delightful!) and warthog droppings (dreadful).

Second, I'd accept that I'm a child in God's grand design. I matter, but He has other people's lives to coordinate too. I'm part of a story that started long ago and will continue to unfold forever. I'm a wisp of smoke that is passing quickly and quietly through this world. My purpose is to share what God has given me: the message of my life.

Third, I wouldn't burden myself with unanswerable questions. Why was I born with privileges and prosperity while Africans face so many obstacles and so few opportunities? Why is this world filled with pain and terrible atrocities? Why do bad things happen to good people? I no longer ask these questions, or wonder why things happen the way they do. To me, questioning life means I'm questioning God himself. When I argue and complain, I'm saying God doesn't know what He's doing.

My season of questioning, struggling, and resisting is over. Now I savor God's gifts while they're here. I enjoy people, relationships, comforts, and good health knowing that each day could be the last. The seasons come and go, but God doesn't.

All Together Now

Our biblical sisters experienced God in different ways and seasons of life. Each woman had a unique, meaningful relationship with Him. Eve walked and talked with the Lord God in the Garden of Eden. Even after being cast out and losing two sons, she continued to depend on Him for blessings.

Sarah's relationship with God evolved over a decade of impatient waiting, wondering, wandering. She and Abraham traveled when God directed, and were blessed with great wealth and descendants as numerous as the stars in the sky. Their servant Hagar had her own personal relationship with God, even talking to the angel of the Lord twice. She gave God a new name: El Roi, or "the God who sees me."

Esther was a leader who lived up to her royal role as queen. She was a smart, strategic woman who didn't rush impulsively into new situations. Naomi, a grieving mother and widow, was more emotional but just as intelligent. She and Ruth followed God home to Israel, to live and prosper with His chosen people.

Martha and her sister, Mary, had loving, face-to-face relationships with Jesus. Martha offered Him the comforts of food, drink, hospitality. Mary gave Him her wholehearted focus, energy, and time.

Mary Magdalene was the first person Jesus chose to see after His resurrection. She was His friend, confidante, and kindred spirit. And finally, we embrace Mary of Nazareth, Jesus' mom, with whom He had a relationship like no other. Nobody in the world knows you like the woman who birthed you, and Mary was His mother. She loved and blessed Him like no other person could.

Let's receive, with the faith of children and the intelligence of women, the blessings in our last Blossom Tip. Let's bring them forward with us, into a new season of hope, faith, and joy.

BRAIN BLOSSOM—
Blessings

I found a childhood picture of me as a toddler, squatting beside a calf at a petting zoo. My hand is resting on the calf's head, and I'm smiling into the camera, eyes squinted against the sun. Today my heart melts when I look at that little Laurie. She had no idea what troubles the world would bring! She also didn't know that God would always be hovering, that she could receive His love, joy, and strength at any time and in every situation. She didn't know Jesus makes the good times better and the bad times easier.

Since little Laurie didn't know what was to come, I wrote her a letter. I told her what she needed to know about people, life, God. I gave her advice for the seasons she'd face, blessing her with love, encouragement, and hope. I told her Jesus is waiting to scoop her into His arms just like a real dad, after she breathes her last and goes home. She doesn't know it, but the best season of her life is yet to come.

What to Do

Choose a picture of yourself as a child—one that makes your heart melt, break, or sing. What do you remember about her? What is she doing? Where was she, what was she wearing, who was she with? Who is missing? What do you love or hate about the picture? What was waiting for that little girl?

Write her a letter, telling her what she needs to know. What do you wish you had known then? Bless her with hope, encouragement, grace, and truth. Give her a Scripture verse to remember, words to cherish. Pray for her. Give her the strength, love, and inspiration she needs to walk through the seasons of her life. Tell her that she will flourish and blossom into who God created her to be . . . one step and one season at a time.

QUESTIONS *for* **JOURNALING** *and* **DISCUSSION**

1. **Saying Yes:** What is the hardest thing God has asked you to accept or do? How did you handle it, and how did it change your relationship with Him?

2. **Becoming You:** On a scale of 1 to 10 (1 = nothing; 10 = everything), how much of "you" do you reveal to the world? What holds you back from becoming—and sharing—more of yourself?

3. **T-Shirts and Totes:** How do you mark seasonal or other transitions in your life? How do you feel about change?

4. **Surprise!** What is the biggest surprise you've ever faced? What did you learn about yourself and others?

5. **Blessings:** What do you miss most about being a little girl? What do you know now that you wish you'd known then?

How do you feel about saying yes to God—and growing forward when you can't go back? If you feel like you're walking alone, come visit me at BlossomTips.com/MaryofNazareth. I'd love to hear from you!

You—Growing Forward

May you experience God's healing, grace, and love as you move forward in your life. May you gain strength and faith from the women who have gone ahead of you. May you share your own story with wisdom and courage.

Above all, may you choose to walk joyfully, humbly, and confidently into the future God has planned for you.

"See, I am doing a new thing! Now it springs up; do you not perceive it? I am making a way in the wilderness and streams in the wasteland" (Isaiah 43:19).

With His love,
Laurie

With Gratitude to

Bruce Kienlen
My mom

The team at Bethany House
Janet Kobobel-Grant

My *She Blossoms* readers!
Without you
there would be no
growing forward.

"May the Lord bless you and
protect you.
May the Lord smile on you and
be gracious to you.
May the Lord show you
His favor
and give you His peace."
—Numbers 6:24–26

xo

NOTES

Introduction

1. Isaiah 43:19.

Chapter 1 Re-creating and Replanting with Eve

1. Marc Cortez, "What Did God Do After Adam and Eve Sinned?" *Transformed*, April 16, 2012, www.westernseminary.edu/transformedblog/2012/04/16/what-did-god-do-after-adam-and-eve-sinned-a-childs-answer-reveals-a-big-problem/. Accessed June 7, 2018.

2. "How do I know which of God's promises are for me?" Got Questions, www.gotquestions.org/God-promises.html. Retrieved March 20, 2018.

3. C. S. Spurgeon, *Morning and Evening* (New Kensington, PA: Whitaker House, 2001), 120.

4. Genesis 4:1.

5. Genesis 4:13 NLT.

6. Isaiah 43:19.

7. Genesis 4:10.

8. Charles H. Dyer, *30 Days in the Land of the Psalms: A Holy Land Devotional* (Chicago: Moody Publishers, 2017), 80.

9. Genesis 4:1.

10. Genesis 4:25.

11. Genesis 4:25.

12. "Eve: The Woman of Unique Distinction," www.biblegateway.com/resources/all-women-bible/Eve.

Chapter 2 Sprouting with Sarah

1. Genesis 16:1.

2. Genesis 17:16; 26:4.

3. "Sarah, Sarai, Sara: The Woman Who Became Mother of Nations," www
.biblegateway.com/resources/all-women-bible/Sarah-Sarai-Sara. Accessed
March 2, 2018.

4. "Sarah, Sarai, Sara."

5. Genesis 1:28.

6. Genesis 16:2.

7. Isaiah 43:19.

8. Genesis 18:11.

9. Genesis 16:4.

10. Genesis 16:6.

Chapter 3 Digging Deeper with Hagar

1. "John Gill's Exposition of the Bible," www.biblestudytools.com/comment
aries/gills-exposition-of-the-bible/genesis-21-15.html. "Hagar: Midrash and
Aggadah," https://jwa.org/encyclopedia/article/hagar-midrash-and-aggadah.
Accessed June 7, 2018.

2. Genesis 13:2, 6.

3. Genesis 16:12.

4. Genesis 16:4 NLT.

5. Genesis 16:6.

6. Genesis 16:7.

7. Genesis 16:13.

8. Genesis 16:7–10.

9. Genesis 16:7.

10. Genesis 21.

11. Isaiah 43:19.

Chapter 4 Uprooting with Naomi

1. "The Ancient Moabites," Bible History Online, www.bible-history.com
/biblestudy/moabites.html.

2. Ruth 1.

3. David Guzik. "Ruth 1—Ruth's Journey," Commentary on Ruth, 2006.
https://enduringword.com/bible-commentary/ruth-1/.

4. Ruth 1:3.

5. Summarized from notes and recall of Canadian Broadcasting Corpora-
tion program.

6. Ruth 1:20–21.

7. Ruth 1:7–9.

8. Genesis 2:18.

9. Ecclesiastes 4:12.

10. Ephesians 1:5.

11. Romans 12:5.

12. Ruth 1:16.

13. Ruth 1:19.
14. Ruth 1:19.

Chapter 5 Starting Fresh with Ruth

1. Ruth 1:13.
2. Ruth 1:20.
3. Oswald Chambers, *My Utmost for His Highest* (Nashville: Thomas Nelson Publishers, 1995), March 20: Friendship with God.
4. Ruth 2:2.
5. Ruth 2:20.
6. Ruth 2:20.
7. Ruth 4:13–14.
8. Ruth 4:21–22.
9. Matthew 1:5.
10. Ruth 4:15.
11. Ruth 2:2.
12. Ruth 2:17.
13. Ruth 2:20.
14. Ruth 3:10–11 (NIV, ESV, KJV, NASB, respectively).

Chapter 6 Growing Roots with Martha and Mary

1. Luke 10:40.
2. Luke 10:41.
3. John 11:21.
4. John 11:32.
5. John 11:35.
6. John 11:33.
7. Ashley Davis Bush, *Transcending Loss: Understanding the Lifelong Impact of Grief and How to Make It Meaningful* (New York: Berkeley Books, 1997), 124.
8. Isaiah 43:19.
9. John 11:38.
10. John 11:39.
11. John 11:44.
12. *She Blossoms* reader comment; name changed to protect privacy.
13. John 11:22.
14. Luke 8:46.

Chapter 7 Reviving Your Heart with Hannah

1. *She Blossoms* reader comment; name and details that follow changed to protect privacy.
2. 1 Samuel 6–7.

3. 1 Samuel 1:8.
4. Anonymous *She Blossoms* reader comment; details changed to protect privacy.
5. 1 Samuel 1:10.
6. 1 Samuel 1:10.
7. 1 Samuel 1:12.
8. 1 Samuel 1:18–19.
9. Proverbs 3:3.
10. Deuteronomy 11:18.
11. Deuteronomy 11:18.
12. Deuteronomy 11:18.
13. 1 Samuel 1:11.
14. Tim Keller, "Hannah's Prayer," sermon, https://gospelinlife.com/down loads/hannah-s-prayer-8819/. Accessed February 6, 2018.
15. 1 Samuel 1:20.

Chapter 8 Renewing Your Purpose with Esther

1. Esther 1.
2. Esther 2.
3. "Keeping Secrets Is Harmful to Your Health, According to New Research from Columbia Business School," www8.gsb.columbia.edu/newsroom/newsn /5187/keeping-secrets-is-harmful-to-your-health-according-to-new-research -from-columbia-business-school. Accessed May 8, 2017.
4. Esther 2:21–23.
5. Esther 3:2–13.
6. Esther 4:11.
7. Esther 4:14.
8. Esther 2:12.
9. Esther 2:8–9.
10. Esther 4–5, 7.
11. Matthew 17:21 and Mark 9:29 KJV and NASB, for example.
12. Leviticus 23:27.
13. Daniel 1:8.
14. 2 Samuel 12:16.
15. Isaiah 43:19.
16. Esther 4:16.
17. James L. Rubart, *The Long Journey to Jake Palmer* (Nashville: Thomas Nelson, 2016), 11.

Chapter 9 Growing Forward with Mary Magdalene

1. Luke 8:2.
2. T. J. Wray, *Good Girls, Bad Girls of the New Testament: Their Enduring Lessons* (Lanham, MD: Rowman & Littlefield, 2016), 90–91.

3. Wray, *Good Girls, Bad Girls of the New Testament*, 90–91.
4. Wray, *Good Girls, Bad Girls of the New Testament*, 82.
5. John 20:17.
6. John 19:30.

Chapter 10 Blossoming into Life with Mary

1. Luke 1:28–29.
2. Matthew 27:46.
3. Luke 2:48–49.
4. John 19:25–27.
5. John 2:1–11.
6. Luke 2:52.
7. Luke 8:19–21.
8. T. J. Wray, *Good Girls, Bad Girls of the New Testament: Their Enduring Lessons* (Lanham, MD: Rowman & Littlefield, 2016), 136.

Laurie Pawlik-Kienlen, creator of the *She Blossoms* blogs and books, lives and writes in her treehouse overlooking Indian Arm in Vancouver, Canada. She holds degrees in psychology and education from the University of Alberta, and a master of social work from the University of British Columbia. Her experiences with a schizophrenic mother, missing father, foster homes, family estrangement, attempted rape, infertility, and three years in Africa taught her that *choosing* to grow forward is essential—especially when you can't go back! Laurie welcomes you at BlossomTips.com.